Race and Gender in the Western Music History S⌐

Race and Gender in the Western Music History Survey: A Teacher's Guide provides concrete information and approaches that will help instructors include women and people of color in the typical music history survey course and the foundational music theory classes. This book provides a reconceptualization of the principles that shape the decisions instructors make when crafting a syllabus. First, it offers new perspectives on canonical composers and pieces that take into account musical, cultural, and social contexts where women and people of color are present. Second, it suggests new topics of study and pieces by composers whose work fits into a more inclusive narrative of music history. The book provides a thematic approach which parallels the traditional chronological sequence in Western music history classes. Three themes include people and communities that suffer from various kinds of exclusion: Locales & Locations; Forms & Factions; Responses & Reception. Each theme is designed to uncover a different cultural facet that is often minimized in traditional music history classrooms but which, if explored, lead to topics in which other perspectives and people can be included organically in the curriculum, while not excluding canonical composers.

Horace J. Maxile, Jr. is Associate Professor of Music Theory at Baylor University. His primary interests are the concert music of Black composers, music semiotics, and gospel music. His research has appeared in scholarly journals such as *Perspectives of New Music, American Music,* the *Journal of the Society for American Music,* and *Black Music Research Journal.*

Kristen M. Turner is a Lecturer in the music and honors departments at North Carolina State University. Her work centers on issues of race, gender, and class in American popular culture at the turn of the twentieth century. Her research has appeared in collected editions and scholarly journals including the *Journal of the American Musicological Society,* the *Journal of the Society for American Music, American Studies,* and *Musical Quarterly.*

Modern Musicology and the College Classroom
Series Editor: James A. Davis, SUNY Fredonia

Modern Musicology and the College Classroom is a series of professional titles for current and future college instructors of musicology in its broadest definition—encompassing music history, ethnomusicology, music theory, and music courses for all majors. Volumes feature a basic introduction to a significant field of current scholarship, a discussion of how the topic impacts pedagogical methodology and materials, and pragmatic suggestions for incorporating these ideas directly into the classroom.

Listening Across Borders
Musicology in the Global Classroom
Edited by James A. Davis and Christopher Lynch

Teaching Electronic Music
Cultural, Creative, and Analytical Perspectives
Edited by Blake Stevens

Race and Gender in the Western Music History Survey
A Teacher's Guide
Horace J. Maxile, Jr. and Kristen M. Turner

Race and Gender in the Western Music History Survey
A Teacher's Guide

Horace J. Maxile, Jr. and Kristen M. Turner

Routledge
Taylor & Francis Group

NEW YORK AND LONDON

First published 2022
by Routledge
605 Third Avenue, New York, NY 10158

and by Routledge
4 Park Square, Milton Park, Abingdon, Oxon, OX14 4RN

Routledge is an imprint of the Taylor & Francis Group, an informa business

© 2022 Taylor & Francis

The right of Horace J. Maxile, Jr. and Kristen M. Turner to be
identified as authors of this work has been asserted in accordance with
sections 77 and 78 of the Copyright, Designs and Patents Act 1988.

Library of Congress Cataloging-in-Publication Data
Names: Maxile, Horace J. Jr., author. | Turner, Kristen M., author.
Title: Race and gender in the Western music history survey : a
teacher's guide / Horace J. Maxile, Jr. and Kristen M. Turner.
Description: [1.] | New York : Routledge, 2022. | Series: Modern
musicology and the college classroom | Includes bibliographical
references and index.
Identifiers: LCCN 2022007870 (print) | LCCN 2022007871 (ebook) |
ISBN 9780367491192 (hardback) | ISBN 9781032313115 (paperback) |
ISBN 9781003044635 (ebook)
Subjects: LCSH: Music--History and criticism. | Music by women
composers—History and criticism. | Music by African American
composers—History and criticism. | Music and race.
Classification: LCC ML193 .M39 2022 (print) | LCC ML193 (ebook) |
DDC 780.89—dc23/eng/20220315
LC record available at https://lccn.loc.gov/2022007870
LC ebook record available at https://lccn.loc.gov/2022007871

ISBN: 978-0-367-49119-2 (hbk)
ISBN: 978-1-032-31311-5 (pbk)
ISBN: 978-1-003-04463-5 (ebk)

DOI: 10.4324/9781003044635

Typeset in Times New Roman
by codeMantra

To those who challenge margins and boundaries by way of pressing from the outside in and from the inside out ...
— Horace

To my parents, Karen and Peter Meyers, life-long educators and my inspiration.
— Kristen

Contents

Illustrations

Acknowledgments

This book began at the suggestion of Jim Davis, our editor, but our partnership originated through the recommendation of Tammy Kernodle. We are grateful to many people for their help, support, and counsel as we labored on the text. We thank Alexandra Apolloni, Peter Askim, Zeynep Bulut, Sarah Gerk, Jill Rogers, Doug Shadle, Rebecca Geoffroy Schwinden, and Kira Thurman for reading portions of the text. Their suggestions enriched and improved our writing and sharpened our thinking about the issues raised when trying to reshape the way we teach Western classical music. Tammy Kernodle and Naomi André organized an exciting workshop on issues of race and gender in music historiography where we first met in 2018. We are inspired by the transformative scholarship, leadership, and friendship provided by Tammy, Naomi, and the other members of the EMRG workshop.

To my wife, Joletta, thank you for your love, support, and patience. To my children, Nathan and Rachel, you are my spark and my inspiration. Dad loves you. To my parents, Horace and Beatrice Maxile, your encouragement and models for life-long learning continue to guide me even to this day. To my brother, Heath, I deeply appreciate you keeping me leveled and light. I thank Baylor University and the School of Music for providing the support and resources to bring this project from conception to completion. Even more so, I thank my Baylor University colleagues Eric Lai, Timothy McKinney, and Edward Taylor for taking the time to contribute to my internal and personal review processes. In addition, a hearty thank you to Gordon Root (SUNY Fredonia) for contributing to the same. Finally, thank you, Kristen. Your administrative skill, critical eye, and congeniality have been instrumental and much appreciated throughout this journey. Many, many thanks for a job well done.

—Horace J. Maxile, Jr.

To my husband, Greg, thank you for your love, for your confidence in me even when I don't believe in myself, and for fixing all my computer problems. My children, Adam, Hannah, and Jacob, had all left the nest by the time Horace and I started writing this book, but they inspire me to take on new challenges as I watch them begin their adult lives. I'm so proud of you and I love you more than I can say. I thank my colleagues at NC State University and the many musicologists who have shaped my thinking over the years through their example as teachers and our conversations about how to serve our students and our discipline better. And finally, thank you Horace. Your good humor, creativity, and ability to conceptualize the big picture when I get bogged down in details have made writing this book a pleasure.

—Kristen M. Turner

Introduction

Teaching is making choices. Teachers choose assignments, grading systems, textbooks, lecture topics, pieces of music, pedagogical approaches....the list goes on. But, perhaps the most important decisions involve WHAT to teach. The critical apparatus by which instructors make these all-important decisions is often unexamined, and may be, in part, beyond an individual's control. What are the institution's goals? What other classes will the students take? What are the students majoring in? What is their musical knowledge? What is required by accrediting bodies? Besides institutional considerations, there are more mundane concerns. What is in the textbook? Whether to use a textbook? What resources are available that are easy to locate? How much time is there to plan the course? What are the teacher's priorities as a musician or scholar? What is the teacher's area of expertise? In the end, whatever decisions an instructor makes when crafting a syllabus, what the students receive is inculcated with a combination of the values of society, the scholarly field, the institution, and the instructor.[1]

In the survey courses on Western classical music that are still the core of many collegiate music programs, too often what results from the combination of all these pressures is a curriculum with a limited perspective that privileges the music, experiences, and voices of white men. Based on topics covered in the major textbooks, our students can be forgiven for thinking that white women simply were not a factor in classical music until relatively recently.[2] As for people of color—they are almost entirely absent except as popular or folk musicians whose work may be presented as a source of inspiration for classical composers, or as practitioners and composers of musical genres that are presented alongside Western classical music. The latter approach, while well meaning, can have the effect of confirming the narrative that art music is the product of white men, while people of color produce popular, vernacular, or "ethnic" music.[3]

DOI: 10.4324/9781003044635-1

Yet any attempt to change the course of study in a class on music in the Western classical tradition is fraught with challenges. There are so many forms of exclusion based on race, class, gender, geography, sexuality, and other factors that it is daunting to imagine how to accumulate enough information to address all these areas. In syllabuses that are already content heavy, how do we integrate new topics in a way that not only accurately reflects the experiences of people living at the time, but also meets the needs of our students as they become music professionals?

Routledge's series of *Teacher's Guides*, of which this volume is one, are designed to bring together recent scholarship and new resources to help instructors fill gaps in their own knowledge and in existing music textbooks about a variety of subjects. We make no attempt in this monograph to address all forms of exclusion. Instead, this volume provides information and pedagogical approaches centered around including white women and people of color in courses on Western classical music.

The survey of Western classical music has a long history of its own. Most musicologists and performers have taken this class themselves in college, and the traditional approach to the course has been enshrined in textbooks that have been through many editions. Changing a course with such an entrenched history is difficult, both conceptually and practically. Some teachers have the luxury of time and institutional support to completely remake their course curriculums to align with the most recent scholarship and progressive pedagogical agendas. For these instructors, this book can provide a road map as well as the resources to redesign the curriculum.

Most people, however, do not have the opportunity, or perhaps even the desire, for sudden, complete change. Instead, they have to make incremental alterations over time, perhaps taking years to fully implement a new course of study that must still work with a textbook or anthology from one of the major academic publishers. This painstaking approach, though time consuming, is the norm and provides an opportunity for change along with stability for students and faculty. Our chapters align with the chronological periodization accepted by the field. The internal organization of each chapter privileges a work-based approach that combines individual compositions with appropriate contextual information, mimicking the organization of most textbooks.

In order to truly diversify or even decolonize the curriculum, we must create a critical apparatus that leads us to include the music and activities of excluded communities and marginalized points of view while also leaving room for canonical works and composers.[4] Without a reconsideration of the values of our curriculum, merely adding new people or topics to the course schedule can degenerate into a kind of tokenism. Music history survey courses are traditionally taught as a history of musical style that follows a seemingly inexorable chronology of one composition's influence on the next until we reach the present. This approach tends to privilege white men because Western society and our methods of scholarly investigation elevate a certain type of musical production (composition over performance or patronage) along with those individuals who moved in circles of influence historically dominated by men. Our reconceptualization rests on two priorities. First, we provide new perspectives on canonical composers and pieces which take into account musical, cultural, and social contexts where women and people of color were present. Second, we offer examples of topics of study and pieces by composers whose work fits into a more inclusive narrative of music history.

In addressing the call for an expanded course content while still aligning with more conventional course designs, this guide offers a thematic approach that also parallels the traditional chronological sequencing in Western music history classes. Our three themes—Locales & Locations, Forms & Factions, and Responses & Reception—are capacious enough to apply to all historical periods and to accommodate instructor-specific goals and topics not covered in these pages. The themes in and of themselves may not appear novel, but they encourage a decentering of conventional narratives in favor of the organic incorporation of sometimes marginalized voices in Western music history courses or in units on classical music.

Locales & Locations

Our treatment of this theme parallels many of the "space and place" concepts in current musicological and ethnomusicological studies.[5] By expanding consideration of *where* music takes place beyond the Western European court chamber, Catholic or Protestant church service, and concert hall, we encounter different music, composers, performers, and cultural contexts that are missed when the geographical focus is narrower. For instance, in the Medieval and Renaissance period, this includes convents or synagogues, or Catholic churches in European colonies or women's courts in Italy during the Baroque period. Outdoor festivals/parks in urban (or rural) areas, private studios, and other non-traditional venues for modern and experimental works can also be considered when evoking this topic. When we find music in new places, we can investigate issues surrounding the marginalization, isolation, and erasure of the music and bodies of white women and people of color. Furthermore, the locales and locations concept could be used by instructors to challenge or support the notion of universality in music, as musical meanings might not transfer entirely from listener to listener, location to location, or era to era. In other words, *where* a piece means can be as important a point of discussion as *how* a piece means or *that* it means at all. Take, for example, Samuel A. Floyd's reconstruction of "myths" and "rituals" regarding the concert hall and music composed for consumption in those venues.[6] Floyd uses the practices and customs associated with performers and patrons of concert music in formal performance venues to analyze how African American composers grapple with the history of racism and their marginalization in American classical music.

Forms & Factions

While opening avenues for drawing attention to elements of musical style or structure, this theme speaks to social and political considerations that often drive the musical composition as well as the suppression of some voices through oppression. In this book, factions are not confined to political dissent within nation-states, principalities, or colonies, but also include those movements and marginalized voices that sought to challenge or expand the musical and artistic norms of their time. The musical analyses in this volume take into account musical parameters such as form, melody, harmony, and rhythm, as well as the external—or extramusical—influences that shape styles, genres, and individual compositions. Disruptions within a style or a genre-specific attribute, no matter how subtle, are sometimes intriguing entry points into the study of a piece and its composer. For our purposes, "forms" should be taken as musical elements in a particular piece in addition to properties and/or conventions that contribute to a style or genre. Harry T. Burleigh's art-song spirituals, for example, are derived from the musical expressions and religious experiences of an enslaved people as well as the imagination of one descendent of slaves who was also Antonin Dvořák's copyist and confidant. The designation "art-song spiritual" implies an accommodation, of sorts, between the two "forms" that preserve the ethos of the source material while also adhering to musical (and performance) conventions associated with the concert hall. In comparison, Joan Tower's *Made in America* uses motives derived from "America the Beautiful" for a suggestive commentary on the beauty that is and that is becoming of America.

The orchestral work features other original tunes and dissonances to disrupt the familiar, patriotic tune, presenting a "musical struggle" that celebrates and questions American identity.[7]

Responses & Reception

It is here that we examine the influences and impacts of four groups that shape musical culture: critics, audiences, patrons, and performers. These groups are slightly different in each period and have different degrees of influence depending upon the specific situation. Conventional music histories tend to privilege these groups only as long as they are undertaken by or support the compositional agendas of white men. Thus, patronage by European nobility from the Middle Ages to the eighteenth century is foregrounded in music history texts, but not the crucial importance of Historically Black Colleges and Universities (HBCUs) for the production and support of music by African American composers. A number of Zenobia Powell Perry's works, for instance, were premiered at Central State University where she served as a faculty member for over 20 years.[8] The patronage of corporations, institutions, and wealthy individuals still contributes to sustaining the performance of Western music, expanding capacities, and creating opportunities for performers. For example, the Sphinx Organization is "dedicated to transforming lives through the power of diversity in the arts," and boasts a robust donor base including The Ford Foundation, J.P. Morgan Chase & Co., and Carlyle Global Partners (among others).[9]

Musical criticism as a journalistic practice began around the middle of the eighteenth century.[10] The privileging of men's voices in publications that featured critiques of music mirrored (and perhaps currently mirrors) the same influences that advanced the formation of the canon. Thus, issues surrounding the location and minimization of critical commentaries by women and people of color throughout the history of Western music fall under this theme. By extension, we also consider positions and roles of audiences as part of Responses & Reception. Performers and composers entertained nobility and provided church music in Europe from the Middle Ages through the eighteenth century, but insights on the practices and preferences of parishioners in colonial centers during the eighteenth century sheds light on the propagation of Western music outside Europe. Considerations of the needs, prejudices, and preferences of audiences, in capacities as mentioned above (and others), afford more nuanced contextual readings that may situate composers as entrepreneurs, engaged citizens, and collaborators.

How to Use This Book

Each chapter opens with a short introduction that decenters the conventional approach to the historical period, highlights information that is generally omitted from textbooks, and explains how the themes apply to that era. Information, composers, and topics that are generally covered in textbooks are often not addressed at all or mentioned only in passing. Paragraphs that address the themes feature examples that instructors could use in their course planning. After the introduction we provide lesson plans and bibliographic content in each chapter. The lesson plans are meant to serve two main priorities. First, they can be implemented immediately to produce a more inclusive curriculum. Each lesson plan contains all the information an instructor needs to add new pieces and new approaches to the canon. Second, they can serve as models which can be adapted to other content areas.

The first lesson plan introduces a piece by a white woman or person of color which is not in any of the major anthologies or textbooks. In addition to basic contextual information, the score and a musical analysis are included. We provide suggestions as to how the piece and composer can be contextualized as a case study for each of the themes and as an example of important musical structures or compositional innovations.

The second lesson plan outlines a new approach to a canonical composer, piece, or repertoire that centers white women or people of color. We believe this type of lesson plan is crucial to a reconceptualization of the course curriculum because it provides examples of ways to reconsider the course material that we already teach. The point of this book is not to leave out Beethoven and Wagner, for that would be as much a distortion of the musical past as it is to omit the work of Marianna Martines or Manuel de Sumaya. We include suggestions for tailoring the content of the lesson to each of the three themes.

After the lesson plans, each chapter includes two bibliographies. The first bibliography is a list of pieces for which both a commercially available recording and a published score exist organized by genre similar to a *Grove*'s work list. We provide web addresses when the recordings or scores are only available through websites such as YouTube or IMSLP.com. Most of the commercial recordings we reference can be accessed through online services such as Spotify, YouTube, or Naxos Online.

The final bibliography contains selected secondary sources on a wide variety of content areas, but rarely includes multiple entries on one topic. Readers can use our citations as the basis of further research as needed. We focus on informational texts over those that center theoretical readings (such as critical race theory or feminist methodologies). Most sources were published recently, but in some content areas, we provide older, foundational texts that offer the basic information needed to inform class lectures. We rarely include sources on composers, pieces, or topics that typically appear in music history texts, even if they refer to minoritized communities. While some of the texts would be suitable for undergraduates, we did not choose references based on that criterion. The bibliography is skewed toward journal articles and essays in collected editions, as they are more limited in scope and quicker to read for course preparation. We sometimes highlight monograph chapters and essays in collected editions or journal special issues based upon what we think might be most useful for instructors and that correspond to that chapter's chronological time period. These suggestions are designed to give readers a sense of the source, not to suggest that other portions of the text would be inappropriate for teaching.

Helpful Hints

- Pay attention to the endnotes! To provide as many sources as possible, we do not replicate citations found in the lesson plans and introductions in the bibliographies.
- The *Oxford Bibliographies* are excellent, curated bibliographies on hundreds of subjects that can be helpful in finding sources on a particular topic.
- We have linked longer bibliographies than could be accommodated in this book through the resources page on the Pedagogy Study Group of the American Musicological Society's website, https://www.teachingmusichistory.com/.
- We have concentrated on printed sources in this book, but there are many websites that provide lesson plans, secondary sources, and primary documents suitable for the classroom including:
  - Digital Resources for Musicology, https://drm.ccarh.org/
  - Inclusive Early Music, https://inclusiveearlymusic.org/
  - Music in the Baroque: Companion Website by Wendy Heller, https://wendyhellerbaroquemusic.com/welcome/towards-a-global-baroque-resources/
  - Beyond Tokenism: Dismantling, Rethinking, Reframing Narratives in Music History Pedagogy, https://musichistoryredo.wordpress.com/
  - Africlassical, https://africlassical.blogspot.com/

Notes

1 Discussions about how to reform, reimagine, or even abandon the music history curriculum have taken place in informal and formal settings for many years. For example, see J. Peter Burkholder, "Curricular Ideas for Music History and Literature," *College Music Symposium* 41 (31 August 2001), https://symposium.music.org/index.php/41/item/3334-curricular-ideas-for-music-history-and-literature. On examining the values inculcated in music education writ large see Barbara Coeyman, "Applications of Feminist Pedagogy to the College Music Major Curriculum: An Introduction to the Issues," *College Music Symposium* 36 (1996): 73–90; Marie McCarthy, "Gendered Discourse and the Construction of Identity: Toward a Liberated Pedagogy in Music Education," *The Journal of Aesthetic Education* 33, no. 4 (Winter 1999): 109–25; Thomas A. Regelski, "Resisting Elephants Lurking in the Music Education Classroom," *Music Educators Journal* 100, no. 4 (June 2014): 77–86. On these issues in the music history survey see: "Roundtable on the Undergraduate Music History Sequence," *Journal of Music History Pedagogy* 5, no. 2 (2015): 49–76. On ways that these issues might play out in the study of American music see "Disciplining American Music Symposium," *American Music* 22, no. 2 (Summer 2004): 270–316.

2 On the challenges of adding women to the western art music course see Cynthia J. Cyrus and Olivia Carter Mather, "Rereading Absence: Women in Medieval and Renaissance Music," *College Music Symposium* 38 (1998): 101–17. For an early defense of adding art music by African Americans in the music history curriculum see Lucius R. Wyatt, "The Inclusion of Concert Music of African-American Composers in Music History Courses," *Black Music Research Journal* 16, no. 2 (Autumn 1996): 239–57.

3 For an example of this approach see Christopher Wilkinson, "Deforming/Reforming the Canon: Challenges of a Multicultural Music History Course," *Black Music Research Journal* (Autumn 1996): 259–77.

4 For the differences between diversifying and decolonizing curriculum see Margaret E. Walker, "Towards a Decolonized Music History Curriculum," *Journal of Music History Pedagogy* 10, no. 1 (2020): 1–19.

5 David B. Knight, *Landscapes in Music: Space, Place, and Time in the World's Great Music* (Lanham, MD: Rowan and Littlefield, 2006). Julie Raimondi's handling of space and place is qualified as a "commonly held understanding" and works well for a richer contrast if we equate space to locale and place to location. "The term 'space' either represents space in the abstract, or else refers to the structural qualities of the physical environment. In opposition, 'place' includes the dimensions of lived experience, or the interaction and use of a space by its inhabitants or users. Place can therefore be thought of as space embedded with meaning." Julie Michelle Raimondi, "Space, Place, and Music in New Orleans" (PhD diss., University of California, Los Angeles, 2012), 6.

6 Samuel A. Floyd, Jr., *The Power of Black Music: Interpreting Its History from Africa to the United States* (New York: Oxford University Press, 1995), 145–51.

7 "Joan Tower," Composer's Notes to *Made in America*. Music Sales Classical, G. Schirmer, http://www.musicsalesclassical.com/composer/work/1605/34003.

8 Jeannie Gayle Pool, *American Composer Zenobia Powell Perry: Race and Gender in the Twentieth Century* (Lanham, MD: The Scarecrow Press, 2009).

9 Sphinx Organization website, http://www.sphinxmusic.org/.

10 *New Grove Dictionary of Music and Musicians*, s.v. "Criticism" (by Winton Dean) (London: Macmillan Publishers Limited, 1980), 37–47.

1 Western Classical Music until 1600

Introduction

Much of the notated music preserved before 1450 in Europe is connected to the Catholic church. Although students might think of Christianity as only thriving in Europe, according to James W. McKinnon's work, the growth of ecclesiastic song and psalmody at the end of the fourth century had its roots in the musical practices of monastic hermits living in loose communities in the Egyptian deserts south of Alexandria. This psalm singing eventually led to the services of the Divine Office.[1] When the Roman Empire fell in the west in 476, Europe lost a significant amount of technical proficiency and humanistic knowledge. While not the Dark Ages of collective memory, medieval Europe was violent and often politically splintered with relatively little contact with the rest of the world. By 720, Arab states controlled what is now Spain and Portugal and later moved into Southern France. The Byzantine Empire extended across modern Turkey and governed coastal areas along the Ionian, Adriatic, and Tyrrhenian Seas, including parts of what is now Rome, Venice, Southern Italy, and Southern Greece. Musical influences from the Arab world made their way into Europe via these routes. Scholars debate the significance and pervasiveness of Arabic influences on European music, but three of the most common European instruments—the rebec, nakers, and lute—originated in the Middle East. Additionally, there are structural and rhyme scheme similarities between Arabic and European song forms including in the *cantiga, rondel,* and *villancico.*[2] In the three religious cultures that mingled in medieval Spain—Jewish, Muslim, and Christian—women seemed to have participated most actively in exclusively oral traditions. Surviving music and poetry suggests that women were viewed with some ambivalence by men, but there are indications

DOI: 10.4324/9781003044635-2

that women were dynamic participants in musical life as singers and instrumentalists.[3]

It is difficult to understand the totality of European women's involvement with music before 1450 because we often do not know composers' names. Secular music likely offered women outlets for composition, improvisation, and performance but very little of this music has survived. As Kimberly Marshall notes, scholarship about this period is inclined to assume that women performed music written by men, but there is little proof for this supposition. Women could have performed their own compositions, and music written by women but transmitted orally could later have been notated by men.[4] The tendency is to treat the female composers we know about, such as Hildegard of Bingen, as exceptional—both as people and in their musical style. However, as Jennifer Bain writes, Hildegard's music was consistent with the traditions of her period.[5] She was also just one of a number of influential women mystics in medieval Christendom. Although we may not always be able to pinpoint the musical activity of medieval nuns, there is no doubt that women were important figures in their religious communities and in Catholic spirituality and theology.[6]

Royal patronage was an important way for women to be involved in musical production before 1450. While women sometimes accompanied their husbands on the crusades to the Holy Land between 1095 and 1291, many aristocratic women were left at home to rule.[7] The study of courtly music and poetry (such as the music of the troubadours and trouvères) helps us to understand ideas about gender, the role of noble women in early modern Europe, and information about individual women and their courts. Fredric L. Cheyette argues that the formulaic language of troubadour poetry eroticized ideas about loyalty in ways that may have strengthened the authority of women rulers.[8] The most famous of the women patrons of lyric poetry and ballads are Eleanor of Aquitaine (c. 1122–1204) and her daughters Marie (Countess of Champagne) and Alix (Countess of Blois).[9] There were many other aristocratic women patrons, some of whom governed in their own names, who might also have been performers, composers, and/or poets but we lack the documentation to understand the extent of these women's musical activities.

After 1450, women continued to be significant patrons of the arts. Court festivals and celebrations (such as weddings or welcoming ceremonies for foreign delegations) were occasions when women servants as well as aristocrats could shine as singers and dancers. Their activities contributed to the political goals of their families and employers.[10]

As was true earlier, some aristocratic families perpetuated a culture of arts patronage for generations which raised the profile and prestige of many women. For example, when Margaret of Austria was Regent of the Netherlands at the beginning of the sixteenth century, she was not only an important diplomatic figure, but also a major patron of the arts. Margaret of Parma, Margaret of Austria's grandniece, was appointed Governor of the Low Countries in 1559 by Philip II. She supported a large musical establishment while fulfilling those duties and continued her musical patronage when she moved to Italy in 1567 where she maintained a court separate from her husband, though she no longer had governing responsibilities.[11] The needs of the patrons in women's courts, however, could be different from that of their male counterparts. Female rulers had to work harder to establish their legitimacy than men, and, for women who maintained separate courts but were not rulers, musical pageantry did not necessarily need to promote diplomatic or political objectives.

Sixteenth-century convents were lively places of music and dramatic entertainment in Europe and home to many women. For instance, in 1552 nuns made up about fifteen percent of all the women living in Florence. Nuns wrote literature and plays on religious subjects and performed music and staged dramas in sometimes elaborate productions throughout the sixteenth century. Lay audiences attended these performances in areas where church officials allowed the practice.[12]

The so-called Age of Exploration began in 1402 when Portuguese sailors discovered and conquered the Canary Islands for the Kingdom of Castile. During the next century, Portuguese and Spanish mariners explored the Atlantic, Indian, and Pacific Oceans, finding routes to India, Africa, and the Americas. Conquest quickly followed trade. European colonies were established in areas all over the world by 1600. With colonization came enslavement and attempts to evangelize and westernize Indigenous and enslaved populations. Christian missionaries taught Indigenous people about church doctrine through prayers or didactic songs, often with texts translated to local languages, and they also recruited local inhabitants (and sometimes enslaved people) as singers and instrumentalists. Much of this music has been lost although some has been preserved including compositions by Spanish-born Hernando Franco whose sixteen *Magnificat* settings are preserved in a choirbook now called the Franco Codex. Indigenous people often assumed their sponsor or mentor's name after they were baptized, so it is sometimes difficult to determine a musician's identity if a native composer shared a European person's name.

Locales & Locations

Although the ability to perform European music was limited in new colonies, in a few areas the church and imperial authorities invested in substantial musical institutions. Franciscan monks and priests from Spain began arriving in Mexico in 1523, just two years after Hernán Cortés conquered the area, and quickly established a religious compound called San Francisco in what would become Mexico City on the site of the Aztec city of Tenochtitlan. Noting that the Nahua people were used to theatricality and music in their religious ceremonies and daily lives, the Franciscans quickly incorporated music and theater in their services and pedagogical activities to aid their evangelization efforts. By 1527, Nahua singers were learning Christian music and performing during the mass and the Divine Office, sometimes accompanied by European and local instruments. Songs with texts in Latin and Nahuatl survive from the sixteenth century including two polyphonic pieces from around 1599 that were written by Hernando Francisco who might have been Nahua.[13] Religious dramas in Nahuatl became so popular and embedded in Nahuatl Catholic life that by the end of the seventeenth century colonial authorities banned them because they diverged so markedly from Spanish traditions. However, these musical plays had become such an important method for the Nahuatl to assert their identity as Indigenous Christians that they ignored the edict and continued writing and performing the works.[14]

Forms & Factions

Musicological and historical investigation into Black people in Europe is in its infancy.[15] Free Black people lived in Europe during the medieval period, but the first Sub-Saharan Africans were captured and taken to Portugal for enslavement in the 1440s. For the next 150 years, most Black people in Europe were enslaved or ex-slaves, and many were not literate. There are records of some diplomatic and religious delegations visiting Europe from Africa in the fifteenth and sixteenth centuries.[16] Blackness could be displayed as part of a theatrical spectacle, and the presence of enslaved Africans in a European court was often a sign of wealth and prestige. By the fifteenth century, there are abundant indications of racialized prejudice and differentiated treatment of Black people by whites. They were positioned within the complex hierarchy of the "other" in Europe that included Jewish and Arabic people for which there were entrenched cultural stereotypes that affected how communities were depicted artistically. Many of the portrayals of Black people in Renaissance art and literature reflect negative stereotypes that still persist, such as sexual promiscuity, laziness, natural musical skill, or the "dim-witted laughing" Black man.[17] A short-lived musical genre called the *moresca* that featured enslaved protagonists developed in sixteenth-century Naples. Designed to be humorous court entertainments, these pieces include street ballads, parodies of madrigals, "comedic" gibberish in the text, and sometimes lewd situations. Scholars have tentatively identified several different influences on this form including an Italian dance from the same time period called the *ballo allo maltese* (which had Moorish characters), some of the stock characters in *commedia dell'arte*, and the *poesía de negros*, a Spanish dramatic verse form.[18] A 1581 collection of Orlando di Lasso's music (*Libro de villanelle, moresche, et altre canzoni a 4, 5, 6 et 8 voci*) includes six *moresche*. With its stereotypical and generally negative depictions of Black people, the *moresca* demonstrates the low social position that they inhabited within the rigidly hierarchical society of sixteenth-century Europe.

Responses & Reception

Early contacts between Europeans and local populations outside of Europe were fraught with tension and danger. Without a common language and similar cultural references, both sides had difficulty communicating and mistrusted each other. Music sometimes played a part in these first encounters but did not necessarily diffuse these meetings.[19] Around 1250, Franciscans and Dominicans began traveling the trade routes to China, following behind Venetian and Genoan merchants. Surviving accounts by Mongols and Europeans show both sides often misunderstood each other and were confused by the other's music because of the unfamiliar timbre, style, and cultural context. Within a century, as contacts between the cultures became more mature and frequent, people became more tolerant of the stylistic differences they heard and were able to see commonalities in the ways they all used music in political and religious circumstances. While the Mongol Empire existed, Europeans were at a tactical and political disadvantage. As the Ottoman Empire gained power in the mid-to-late fourteenth century, significant contact between Europe and Asia largely ended until the sixteenth century by which time the global situation had changed yet again. Buoyed by the wealth of their colonies, Europeans usually assumed a dominant position in subsequent encounters.[20]

Notes

1 James W. McKinnon, "Desert Monasticism and the Later Fourth-Century Psalmodic Movement," *Music & Letters* 75, no. 4 (1994): 505–21.

2 David Wulstan, "Boys, Women and Drunkards: Hispano-Mauresque Influences on European Song?" in *The Arab Influence in Medieval Europe*, ed. Dionisius A. Agius and Richard Hitchcock (Reading: Ithaca Press, 1994), 136–67.

3 Judith R. Cohen, "*Ca no soe joglaresa:* Women and Music in Medieval Spain's Three Cultures," in *Medieval Woman's Song: Cross-Cultural Approaches*, ed. Anne L. Klinck and Ann Marie Rasmussen (Philadelphia: University of Pennsylvania Press, 2002), 66–80, at 78.

4 Kimberly Marshall, "Symbols, Performers, and Sponsors: Female Musical Creators in the Late Middle Ages," in *Rediscovering the Muses: Women's Musical Traditions*, ed. Kimberly Marshall (Boston: Northeastern University Press, 1993), 140–68, at 158.

5 Jennifer Bain, "Hildegard, Hermannus, and Late Chant Style," *Journal of Music Theory* 52, no. 1 (2008): 123–49.

6 For examples see Katherine Gill, "Open Monasteries for Women in Late Medieval and Early Modern Italy: Two Roman Examples," in *The Crannied Wall: Women, Religion, and the Arts in Early Modern Europe*, ed. Craig A. Monson (Ann Arbor: University of Michigan Press, 1992), 15–48; John A. Nichols and Lillian Thomas Shank, eds. *Medieval Religious Women*, vol. 1, *Distant Echoes* (Kalamazoo, MI: Cistercian Publications, 1984).

7 Matilda Tomaryn Bruckner, "Fictions of the Female Voice: The Women Troubadours," in *Medieval Woman's Song: Cross-Cultural Approaches*, ed. Anne L. Klinck and Ann Marie Rasmussen (Philadelphia: University of Pennsylvania Press, 2002), 127–51, at 130.

8 Fredric L. Cheyette, "Women, Poets, and Politics in Occitania," in *Aristocratic Women in Medieval France*, ed. Theodore Evergates (Philadelphia: University of Pennsylvania Press, 1999), 138–78.

9 Rebecca A. Baltzer, "Music in the Life and Times of Eleanor of Aquitaine," in *Eleanor of Aquitaine: Patron and Politician*, ed. William W. Kibler (Austin: University of Texas Press, 1976), 61–80.

10 For one example of this combination of music and diplomacy see Judith Bryce, "Performing for Strangers: Women, Dance, and Music in Quattrocento Florence," *Renaissance Quarterly* 54, no. 4 (2001): 1074–1107.

11 Seishiro Niwa, "'Madama' Margaret of Parma's Patronage of Music," *Early Music* 33, no. 1 (2005): 25–37.

12 Elissa B. Weaver, "Spiritual Fun: A Study of Sixteenth-Century Tuscan Convent Theater," in *Women in the Middle Ages and the Renaissance: Literary and Historical Perspectives*, ed. Mary Beth Rose (Syracuse, NY: Syracuse University Press, 1986), 173–206.

13 These songs were long attributed to Hernando Franco, but many scholars now believe that they were written by an Indigenous person who took Franco's name upon baptism. Jonathan Truitt refers to this composer as Hernando Francisco in his work on this repertoire. Jonathan Truitt, "Adopted Pedagogies: Nahua Incorporation of European Music and Theater in Colonial Mexico City," *The Americas* 66, no. 3 (2010): 311–30.

14 This paragraph is based on Truitt, "Adopted Pedagogies."

15 See *Black Central Europe* (https://blackcentraleurope.com/) for an overview of scholarship in the field.

16 Kate Lowe, "Introduction: The Black African Presence in Renaissance Europe," in *Black Africans in Renaissance Europe*, ed. Thomas Foster Earle and K.J.P. Lowe (Cambridge: Cambridge University Press, 2005), 1–14, at 2.

17 Kate Lowe, "The Stereotyping of Black Africans in Renaissance Europe," in *Black Africans in Renaissance Europe*, ed. Thomas Foster Earle and K.J.P. Lowe (Cambridge: Cambridge University Press, 2005), 17–47.

18 Natalie Operstein, "Golden Age *Poesía de Negros* and Orlando di Lasso's *Moresche*: A Possible Connection," *Romance Notes* 52, no. 1 (2012): 13–18.

19 David Smith, "Colonial Encounters through the Prism of Music: A Southern African Perspective," *International Review of the Aesthetics and Sociology of Music* 33, no. 1 (2002): 31–55.

20 Jason Stoessel, "Voice and Song in Early Encounters Between Latins, Mongols, and Persians, ca. 1250–ca. 1350," in *Studies on a Global History of Music: A Balzan Musicology Project*, ed. Reinhard Strohm (London: Routledge, 2018), 83–113.

Lesson 1.1: Vittoria Aleotti, "Hor che la vaga Aurora"

Background

Italian composer Vittoria Aleotti (c1575–after 1620) was born into a family that valued music and music education. There is some speculation as to whether Vittoria and another Aleotti composer, Rafaella, are the same person.[1] Much of what is known about Vittoria comes by way of a dedication written by her father, engineer and architect, Giovanni Battista Aleotti. The dedication accompanies Vittoria's collection of madrigals, *Ghirlanda de madrigali a quatro voci*, published in 1593.[2] C. Ann Carruthers, the editor of *Ghirlanda de madrigali,* notes that Vittoria demonstrated interest in music as a young child when she observed her older sister's music lessons. Because of her quick development and growing skill, her instructors suggested that Vittoria be sent to the convent of San Vito for further study.[3] Her father agreed with this because of the superb musicianship of the women in the convent as well as the quality of the ensembles. It was Vittoria's father who arranged for the collection of madrigals to be published after she entered the convent. According to Suzanne Cusick, the madrigals in the collection "represent a range of late 16th-century styles, from simple canzonettas to serious efforts at exploiting dissonance to express images of amorous longing or distress."[4] It is remarkable that the madrigal collection was published when Aleotti was still a teenager.

The publication reveals her developing technique and the potential of a budding composer.

As Giovanni Aleotti's dedication is the primary source of information on Vittoria, much of what scholars believe about her life and accomplishments is gleaned from examinations of historical and social contexts involving her father as well as the status of women musicians in Italy during the late sixteenth century.

"Hor che la vaga Aurora"

Vittoria Aleotti's madrigal "Hor che la vaga Aurora" is the first piece in the collection *Ghirlanda de madrigali a quarto voci*.[5] The composer's use of suspensions at cadential points and suggestive use of word painting in polyphonic and homophonic textures situates the piece as a conventional example of madrigals that were common during the sixteenth century. Although primarily set in a G mode, Aleotti occasionally emphasizes other notes in the mode (such as D and C) with cadences.[6] The poetic text summons mythological subjects and symbols such as Aurora (the dawn), Apollo (the son of Latona), and Apollo's lyre, as reflective of the beauty and hope of the sunrise and the sounds of a new day. Serving as a point of reference for the following commentary, the English translation of the text appears below:

> Now that lovely Dawn
> riding on a fiery chariot
> appears everywhere
> with Latona's son,
> and shows her flaxen hair
> to the Alps and to the
> countryside near us,
> with sweet tones
> he plays his well-tuned lyre,
> so that wandering spirits listen intently
> to the harmony
> that lifts and sends
> our souls heavenward.[7]

Aleotti opens with a pair of "imitative duos" between the alto/soprano and tenor/bass voices, respectively.[8] In noting the cross-relation between the F and F# in the opening measures, one might surmise that Aleotti wanted the subject to have a strong, half-step arrival to the final (G). Imitating at the fifth above the initial statement, the answer in the soprano is tonal and its adjusted ending hints toward C in measures 5 and 6. C is not a strong arrival, however, as the first duo dovetails with the entrance of the second duo. The bass enters with literal restatement on G and the tenor enters a fifth above with a real answer and a half-step arrival to D. However, when C# is introduced in measure 9, F-natural is Aleotti's choice until the cadence in measure 13. This lends toward brief encounters with D minor sonorities before the F# arrives. Aleotti's contrapuntal treatments after the entrance of the tenor are rather free, overlapping phrases and borrowing material from the subject until the cadence in measure 13.

A more homophonic texture ensues at measure 14, as the beams from the "fiery chariot" highlight arrivals on both G (m. 15) and C (m.17), but the setting of "appears everywhere" or *"Appar in ogni loco"* interrupts the homophony. The voices, as early as measure 15, begin to appear everywhere on that text, subtly activating more polyphony. The first statement, in the soprano, is overlapped with the concluding homophonic statement of *"Sovra un caro di foco."* While melodic ideas associated with *"Sovra"* are stated between the voices, so are imitative statements of *"Appar in ogni"* in the bass, alto, and tenor voices, respectively. When Latona's son is invoked, Aleotti returns to a homophonic texture. Aleotti's assertion on F-natural in the bass complicates the cadence on D in measure 32. Our first significant arrival on D was in measure 13 on the word *Aurora* or "Dawn" and the sonority was affected with the F# at the cadence. Now the Dawn's flaxen hair is symbolically tied to Apollo and his chariot in measure 32, and the missing third of the D chord somewhat mystifies her bright, radiant beams. This moment is heightened by a prolonged 4–3 suspension in measure 31, where the preparing sonority is also a D chord with no third.

Aleotti's word painting is deliberate and descriptive in her handling of the "Alps" and "countryside." In measures 32 through 34, statements of *"Alpi"* in all voices leap upward. The most dramatic leap, a perfect fifth, is in the tenor voice. The treatments of rhythm and imitative textures are key at this moment, as the leaping gesture in three of the four voices is prepared with a rest. The rests along with the imitative entrances at short time intervals create a terraced effect, evocative of a mountain range. Indeed, the contrasting and compelling depictions of "countryside" feature downward leaps in all but one voice. In approaching the cadences on G in measure 42 and C in measure 46, chains of colorful suspensions come by way of the stepwise motion in the upper voices. Because of how they are prepared, they are referred to as "consonant fourth" (4–3) suspensions.[9] Aleotti's word-painting technique continues with depictions of the types of parallel sonorities that would result from shifts up and down the fingerboard of a lute or the simultaneous plucked strings of a harp.[10] Parallel tenths and sixths are predominately used for each setting of text that addresses Apollo's "well-tuned lyre." Also noteworthy are the additions of accidentals, particularly the B♭s in the tenor and bass (from the soft hexachord) before the F♯ (mm. 52–53).[11]

Homophony returns when Apollo plays "so that wandering spirits listen intently." One final utterance of F-natural occurs before settling on F♯ for the remainder of the piece. The last statement of F-natural occurs around the "wandering spirit" in measure 58. Whereas the following cadences on G are heightened with the F♯s, this setting may be related more so to the previous arrival on C which is not the final. Additionally, the F-natural also appears as part of a 6/3 sonority that is part of a sequential chain that ultimately lands on the final, G. Thus, "the harmony that lifts our souls" is an ultimate resting in G with a lilting, concluding episode in a triple meter (mm. 60–76).

Locales & Locations

Whereas Vittoria is believed to have grown musically through her studies and exposure to other women musicians in the convent of San Vito, it is the financial and social status of her father Giovanni Aleotti within the court of Ferrara that likely provided the resources for private study. As Jane Bower observes "many [women composers] came from noble, patrician, and professional families that could afford private tutors for their daughters."[12] Because of early successes with projects in Ferrara, Giovanni was named the chief architect in Ferrara in 1571. While earning a salary in that position, Giovanni also accepted other commissions and projects as approved by the Duke.[13] He published technical treatises and designed a new theater in Ferrara around 1604–06. Poet and dramatist Giovanni Battista Guarini valued Aleotti's skill in these areas as well, and their friendship developed out of a mutual respect for the other's professional work in the court.[14] C. Ann Carruthers suspects that this relationship allowed Vittoria to acquire the Guarini poems she set in the madrigal collection.

Further Consideration: Consider the areas of citizenry and other courtly appointments that could have come by way of Giovanni Aleotti's professional skill. As there are some texts attributed to anonymous authors in Vittoria's collections, is it safe to speculate that Giovanni's connections provided access to texts by authors less prominent than Guarini?

Forms & Factions

Considering the limited number of opportunities for women musicians in Italy in the sixteenth century, Vittoria Aleotti's achievement as a published composer situates her and a few other women composers as a faction of sorts—not as an organized group of dissenters to societal norms, but as a loosely tethered tradition of creative musicians who worked in the margins of musical cultures that were predominately male. This is not to say that women did not have any opportunities to perform. Some women gained opportunities as singers through ensembles that developed around 1580 (usually called *concerto delle donne*), and there was also significant musical activity (and instruction) in the convents.[15] Given her distinctive abilities and possible exposure to musical women in sacred and secular spaces, Vittoria's interest in composition, though unusual, appears to follow a sensible trajectory of creative endeavors for a young musician. It is not known whether she was aware of the limited output of other women composers such as Maddalena Casulana, Paola Massarenghi of Parma, or Cesarina Ricci de Tingoli, but her madrigals place her among the earliest published women composers in the western tradition.[16]

Further Consideration: Did Vittoria Aleotti's accomplishments in composition lead to improved conditions for women musicians in general? Students can be challenged here to think about the role of the church in society and the role of women in the church, as well as whether success by one woman could lead to an increased respect for all women. Would acceptance as secular entertainers translate to respect for their talents and/or personhood?

Responses & Reception

As a composer, Vittoria Aleotti's name first appears in a 1591 anthology of madrigals by composers that were active in Ferrara. Although referred to as "Vittorio" in the collection, scholars attribute the work to Vittoria. Aleotti's inclusion "in a publication containing works by such Ferrarese luminaires as Pasquini and Agostini attests to the esteem in which the young composer—then not more than sixteen years old—was held."[17] Venetian publisher Giacomo Vincenzi printed the 1591 anthology as well as *Ghirlanda de madrigali*. Carruthers speculates that Giovanni Aleotti wanted to capitalize on the prestige of Venetian printing houses and their access to wider distribution networks when he turned to Vincenzi rather than a publisher in Ferrara. Carruthers noted Vincenzi's overall printing work as average, but "in Vittoria Aleotti's *Ghirlanda* we find evidence of what was, for Vincenzi, unusual care: there seems to be relatively few errors."[18]

Further Consideration: Considering the reasonable success of Vincenzi in the field of publishing with middling production standards, why did Vincenzi take "unusual care" with Vittoria Aleotti's collection? Students could be encouraged to think about matters related to business relationships (impressing Giovanni Aleotti and Ferrarese nobility) or the possibility that Vincenzi realized the uniqueness of an opportunity to publish a collection of madrigals by a young lady still in her teenage years.

1. Hor che la vaga Aurora

Vittoria Aleotti, "Hor che la vaga Aurora" from *Music at the Courts of Italy*, Vol. 1, edited by C. Ann Carruthers © 1994 by Broude Brothers Ltd. Used with permission by C. F. Peters Corporation. All rights reserved.

2

1) Source: "Appar in ogni loco Co'l figlio di Latona"

4

2) Source: minim

6

Notes

1 Vittoria Aleotti, *Ghirlanda de Madrigali a Quatro Voci*, ed. C. Ann Carruthers (New York: The Broude Trust, 1994), xvii–xx. Carruthers, in theorizing that Vittoria may have adopted the name Rafaella upon entering the convent, discusses lacunae, facts, and circumstantial evidence that fortify the claim, noting on page xvii "nothing is known of Vittoria after 1593, and nothing of Rafaella before 1592."

2 Aleotti, *Ghirlanda de Madrigali a Quatro Voci*, xiii–iv.

3 Jane Bowers, "The Emergence of Women Composers in Italy, 1566–1700," in *Women Making Music: The Western Art Tradition, 1150–1950*, ed. Jane Bowers and Judith Tick (Urbana: University of Illinois Press, 1986), 129.

4 Suzanne Cusick, "Aleotti, Vittoria," *Grove Music Online*.

5 Aleotti, *Ghirlanda de Madrigali a Quatro Voci*, 103.

6 Aleotti, *Ghirlanda de Madrigali a Quatro Voci*, xxviii. In an outline of editorial policies for the Aleotti volume, Carruthers confirms that "all accidentals that appear in the staff in this edition also appear in the original source; the only concession to modern practice is the use of a natural, instead of a sharp, to cancel a flat or to indicate that the relevant pitch is to be sung as *mi*." The score is comprised of scanned images from the Carruthers edition.

7 Aleotti, *Ghirlanda de Madrigali a Quatro Voci*, 103.

8 Peter Schubert, *Modal Counterpoint, Renaissance Style*, 2nd Edition (New York: Oxford University Press, 2008), 276. Chapter 19 provides commentary on matters of structure in Renaissance works that use four voices. Of the three types of structures outlined by Schubert, Aleotti's piece aligns most readily with his "pair of imitative duos" formal design.

9 Thomas Benjamin, *The Craft of Modal Counterpoint: A Practical Approach* (New York: Routledge, 2005), 98. In this type of suspension, "the fourth … falls on a weak beat, is approached by step (usually from above), and is followed immediately by a 4-3 suspension over the dominant note in the lowest voice."

10 It is not known whether Aleotti knew about the performance capabilities of a Greek lyre or if she owned one, but it is safe to assume that she was aware of the lute.

11 Renaissance theory was influenced by a hexachordal solmization system that was related to the medieval chant/pitch system. There are three basic hexachords: hard, natural, and soft. G is the final in the Aleotti and the hexachords are: hard (G-A-B-C-D-E), natural (C-D-E-F-G-A), and soft (G-A-*Bb*-C-D-E). See Margaret Bent and Alexander Silbiger, "Musica ficta," *Grove Music Online*. See also Schubert, *Modal Counterpoint*, 334–37.

12 Bowers, "The Emergence of Women Composers in Italy, 1566–1700," 131–32.

13 Aleotti, *Ghirlanda de Madrigali a Quatro Voci*, x–xxi.

14 Aleotti, *Ghirlanda de Madrigali a Quatro Voci*, xxi.

15 Bowers, "The Emergence of Women Composers in Italy, 1566–1700," 121–28. For more on the *concerto delle donne*, see also Anthony Newcomb, "Courtesans, Muses, or Musicians? Professional Women Musicians in Sixteenth-Century Italy," in *Women Making Music: The Western Art Tradition, 1150–1950*, ed. Jane Bowers and Judith Tick (Urbana: University of Illinois Press, 1986), 90–115.

16 Bowers, "The Emergence of Women Composers in Italy, 1566–1700," 117.
17 Aleotti, *Ghirlanda de Madrigali a Quatro Voci*, xiii.
18 Aleotti, *Ghirlanda de Madrigali a Quatro Voci*, xxiii–xxv.

Lesson 1.2: The *Cantigas de Santa Maria* and the Arabic Influence on Western Art Music

Background

The major music history textbooks mention the *Cantigas de Santa Maria* of Alfonso X "the Learned" of Castile (1221–84, ruled 1252–84) in passing, but they do not go into the same detail about these songs as the French secular song repertoire. The *Cantigas* are one of the largest extant collections of medieval song. Researchers have studied the manuscripts' illustrations and texts to gain insights into the daily life of people from the era and to understand Alfonso X's theology and his foreign and domestic political objectives. The purpose of this lesson is to show the various ways that Arabic influence was crucial to medieval European history and arts, as well as to provide an example that complements the themes of "courtly love" reflected in the repertoire of the troubadours and trouvères.

The Iberian Peninsula was at the crossroads of Islam, Judaism, and Christianity during the thirteenth century. Alfonso X was a renowned intellectual who filled his court with scholars from all three religious backgrounds. It is unclear how many of the 427 *Cantigas de Santa María* he wrote, but he spent over thirty years supervising their creation.[1] Four manuscripts preserve the repertoire, with three featuring elaborate illustrations.[2] A collection of devotional songs in Portuguese-Galician (the language of lyric poetry in thirteenth-century Spain), the *Cantiga* texts are dedicated to the Virgin Mary and all but seventeen describe miracles made possible through her intervention; the others are Marian songs of praise. They were probably intended for services celebrating the Virgin Mary and as court entertainment. The texts often portray commonplace situations and individuals (traveling merchants or pilgrims, physicians treating patients, criminals being punished, etc.) who experience the Virgin's miraculous intercession. Although the poems vary drastically in length and use many different metrical schemes, many are in the *zajal* poetic form which originated in Muslim Spain, and virtually all contain a refrain, which may have been sung by a chorus with a soloist performing the verses. Scholars believe that the monophonic tunes notated in the manuscripts were pre-existent secular melodies.

In 1922, Julián Ribera published a partial musical transcription of the *Cantigas* which he interpreted as classical Arab melodies. To conform to his ideas about typical Arab music, Ribera often ignored the notation in the scores, causing musicologists to roundly criticize his edition and reject an Arabic origin or influence on the repertoire.[3] More recently, however, scholars have re-examined the connections between the *Cantigas* and Moorish-Andalusian (or Ibero-Arab) musical traditions. (Al-Andalus refers to the areas of present-day Spain and Portugal ruled by Muslims between 711 and 1492.)

Manuel Pedro Ferreira notes that the musical form of many of the *Cantigas* corresponds to the French *virelai* and the Moorish-Andalusian *muwashshah* which have the same structure (AbbaA). There are examples of the *muwashshah* from c. 1100, while the first *virelai* date from c. 1300, thus it is more likely that the *Cantigas* were influenced by the *muwashshah*.[4] Scholars have also struggled to understand the rhythmic notation used in the *Cantiga* manuscripts which seem to be connected to Notre Dame polyphony but are not truly in Franconian notation.[5]

Ferreira claims that many of the *Cantiga's* rhythms resemble Arabic rhythmic cycles; a view not shared by David Wulston who sees few similarities to Arabic rhythms. Instead, he reads the rhythms as being a unique confluence of Hispanic and Arabic sources, perhaps most closely related to Ionic rhythms that date back to Greek and Roman times and were typically used for erotic dances.[6] Wulston believes that the *Cantigas* are transcriptions of an otherwise oral tradition that is most closely related to instrumental dance music rather than chant, other medieval song repertories, or strictly Arabic sources. He also observes that melodically most of the *Cantigas* are not written in the ecclesiastic modes used by Gregorian chant, which he sees as proof that the tunes come out of secular oral traditions instead of worship music.[7]

The particulars of the scholarly arguments about the antecedents of and influences on the *Cantigas* is perhaps less important than the insight that the *Cantigas*, as well as the troubadour/trouvère repertoire, developed in a cultural milieu with a significant oral musical tradition and was far more diverse ethnically and religiously than we might imagine. The debate over the *Cantigas'* origins is partially a result of the incomplete archive, but also reflects scholarly reluctance to accept or study the presence and influence of people of color and their music in Europe.[8]

Locales & Locations

Alfonso X's court was a cultured, intellectual, and diverse seat of power and learning. He attracted Catholic, Muslim, and Jewish scholars that contributed to an impressive amount of intellectual production in law, history, music, art, language, and literature. Alfonso X was more than a patron, he was an enthusiastic contributor to many of the scholarly and artistic projects that came out of his court. The *Cantigas de Santa Maria* are a landmark in music, literature, and art (via the illuminations). He and his court also innovated in astronomy, wrote a legal code that is fundamental to United States law as well as in many other parts of the globe, helped advance and establish the Castilian language (and vernacular languages in general) over Latin for secular and governmental use, and changed historical writing to include cultural and social topics instead of solely focusing on political chronicles. In all these endeavors, he was deeply influenced by Islamic culture and learning. Because of Castile's proximity to Iberian areas under Muslim control, it would be tempting to think of Alfonso's court as unique in Europe. But this is not the case. Holy Roman Emperor Frederick II (1194–1250) maintained a court with a significant Muslim presence, the medical breakthroughs in Montpellier as well as the arts of Southern France relied on Islamic influence, as did the mathematical innovations in Pisa and the philosophical and theological ideas of Thomas Aquinas and Francis of Assisi. Robert I. Burns writes,

> Alfonso is not a freak or a break with European tradition... It is more true to say that we moderns broke with him, when the northern industrial countries of the early nineteenth century invented a nationalist historiography that moved Europe's medieval center north to jibe with its more modern center and marginalized the heartlands of its earlier Mediterranean-centered self. As we recapture our wider history in our day, Alfonso the Learned can be seen as a major actor in a widely based transfer of learning and letters from Islam to the West.[9]

Further Consideration: Challenge students to think about why the history of people of color and non-Christian people in Europe has been erased or minimized. How does knowing the history of the *Cantigas* change their perception of medieval Europe?

Forms & Factions

Beginning in 1095 and continuing for centuries, European rulers and the Catholic church supported and conducted a series of religious wars called the Crusades to claim land from Muslim rulers. While the most famous of these were intended to liberate Jerusalem from Islamic control (fought between 1095 and 1291), there were crusades to Christianize other areas or to eliminate what papal authorities thought were heretical Christian sects in parts of Europe. Alfonso X had direct connections to the *Reconquista*, the centuries-long effort by Christians to re-take the Iberian Peninsula. His great-grandfather, Alfonso VIII, won the decisive Battle of Las Navas de Tolosa in 1212 and his father, Fernando III, won control of many Spanish Islamic cities. Alfonso X took part in the battles that his father won in Murcia and Seville. Throughout his reign, Alfonso X and the Catholic church considered his military activities to maintain control of the cities his father conquered, as well as to extend Castilian domination in the area, as part of the Crusades. As important as the *Cantigas* are as devotional poetry, they were also part of Alfonso X's self-representation and reflected his political objectives. The *Cantigas* were probably performed in churches and at court wherever Alfonso was in residence. Never a passive onlooker, the lavish illuminations show Alfonso directly overseeing the production of the *Cantiga* manuscripts and dictating the texts, emphasizing his personal piety and artistic prowess. The illustrations of the Marian praise songs fuse Alfonso's earthly authority with his spiritual leadership, as he is the only human who shares the Virgin's timeless and heavenly space in the illuminations.[10] Edward Holt argues that the depictions of Mary in the texts of many of the *Cantigas* are consistent with what he calls a "crusading spirituality." They include portrayals of the Virgin as a military patron, which supported Alfonso's crusading order honoring Mary, and emphasizing Mary's role in the remission of sins and promoting the faith—two reasons the church used to justify the Crusades.[11]

Further Consideration: The Provençal secular repertoire and the *Cantigas* are two of the most extensive collections of music to survive from the thirteenth and fourteenth centuries. Discuss how the repertoires complement each other and provide different kinds of information about medieval life and music.

Responses & Reception

Even as musicologists have argued about the extent of Arabic influence on the *Cantigas*, performers have responded to the European Early Music movement's need for "authenticity" by integrating many elements of modern Andalusian performance practice when interpreting the repertoire. There is a dynamic living Andalusian music scene, but no extant medieval Arabic poetic sources with musical notation. Additionally, there are only a handful of surviving medieval Arabic instruments (all percussion), and only a few extant documents that describe the region's musical practice. Western recordings of the *Cantigas* and other medieval song repertoires, along with *muwashshah* and *zajal* texts performed with newly composed musical accompaniments (what Dwight Reynolds calls "medievalized settings"), draw upon modern Andalusian and Moroccan traditions, and use instruments from the medieval period sometimes modeled after the *Cantigas'* illuminations. These historically informed recordings can never be more than guesses. With only melodic notation that has contested rhythmic meanings to guide them, recordings of the *Cantigas* are dramatically different from each other depending upon the interpretive choices of the performers. Dwight Reynolds claims that using imagined medieval Andalusian techniques was a political statement for some musicians who innovated this style in the 1970s. These interpretations re-connected Spain with the Middle East and celebrated a suppressed aspect of Iberian history.[12] Meanwhile, John Haines associates the use of Arabic style in contemporary medieval performance to European fascination with the Middle East that stretches back to nineteenth-century orientalism rather than political motivations.[13]

Further Consideration: Although this example reveals the extent to which Early Music performers must fill in the blanks of the historical record when interpreting medieval music, all scores leave out vital information. Using any piece of notated music, work with students to create a list of what the score tells them and what it does not. Then, compare an old recording of one piece with a very recent recording to show how vocal and instrumental techniques and interpretations have changed in the last one hundred years. The goal is to make clear how our perception of musical style and performance practice is a cultural construction that changes over time.

Notes

1 John Esten Keller and Annette Grant Cash, *Daily Life Depicted in the Cantigas de Santa Maria* (Lexington: University Press of Kentucky, 1998), 1.
2 Links to digital copies of the manuscripts available online can be accessed through *The Cantigas de Santa Maria: Facsimiles*, http://www.pbm.com/~lindahl/cantigas/facsimiles/
3 Manuel Pedro Ferreira, "Andalusian Music and the *Cantigas de Santa Maria*," in *Cobras e son: Papers on the Text, Music and Manuscripts of the Cantigas de Santa Maria*, ed. Stephen Parkinson (Oxford: European Humanities Research Centre of the University of Oxford, 2000), 7–19, at 7.
4 See Manuel Pedro Ferreira, "Rondeau and Virelai: The Music of Andalus and the *Cantigas de Santa Maria*," *Plainsong and Medieval Music* 13, no. 2 (2004): 127–40, for a concise explanation of the *zajal* and *muwashshah*, as well as his argument for linking the *muwashshah* to the *Cantigas*. Scholars disagree whether the *virelai* and *ballade* developed essentially independently of the *muwashshah* and *zajal*, or if they are musical descendants of the Arabic forms. Some musicologists cite the lack of medieval-era manuscripts of Arabic music to justify seeing connection between Arabic and French secular song as speculative at best. See Jozef Pacholczyk, "The Relationship Between the Nawba of Morocco and the Music of the Troubadours and Trouvères," *The World of Music* 25, no. 2 (1983): 5–16.

5 See Manuel Pedro Ferreira, "Rhythmic Paradigms in the *Cantigas de Santa Maria*: French versus Arabic Precedent," *Plainsong and Medieval Music* 24, no. 1 (2015): 1–24, for an overview of the scholarship on rhythm in the *Cantigas*.

6 David Wulstan, "Bring on the Dancing-Girls! (*a Gadibus usque auroram*)," *Al-Masāq* 17, no. 2 (2005): 221–49.

7 David Wulstan, "A Pretty Paella: The Alfonsine *Cantigas de Santa Maria* and their Connexions with Other Repertories," *Al-Masāq* 21, no. 2 (2009): 191–227.

8 Kate Lowe, "Introduction: The Black African Presence in Renaissance Europe," in *Black Africans in Renaissance Europe*, ed. Thomas Foster Earle and K.J.P. Lowe (Cambridge: Cambridge University Press, 2005), 3.

9 This paragraph is based on Robert I. Burns, "*Stupor Mundi*: Alfonso X of Castile, the Learned," in *Emperor of Culture: Alfonso X the Learned of Castile and His Thirteenth-Century Renaissance*, ed. Robert I. Burns (Philadelphia: University of Pennsylvania Press, 1990), 1–13; quotation from page 13.

10 George D. Greenia, "The Politics of Piety: Manuscript Illumination and Narration in the *Cantigas de Santa Maria*," *Hispanic Review* 61, no. 3 (1993): 325–44.

11 Edward Lawrence Holt, "Cantigas de Santa María, Cantigas de Cruzada: Reflections of Crusading Spirituality in Alfonso X's *Cantigas de Santa María*," *Al-Masāq* 27, no. 3 (2015): 207–24.

12 Dwight Reynolds, "The Re-creation of Medieval Arabo-Andalusian Music in Modern Performance," *Al-Masāq* 21, no 2 (2009): 175–89.

13 John Haines, "The Arabic Style of Performing Medieval Music," *Early Music* 29, no. 3 (2001): 369–78.

Bibliography

Score/Recording

Secular Vocal

Anonymous (music); Marguerite of Austria (text). "Me fauldra il tousjours ainsi languir"; "Se je souspire/Ecce iterum." In *The Chanson Albums of Marguerite of Austria*, edited by Martin Picker. Berkeley: University of California Press, 1965.

• La Morra. *Dame de Deuil: Musical Offerings for Marguerite of Austria*, 2005.

Aleotti, Vittoria (also Raffaella). "Hor che la vaga Aurora"; "Cor mio perche pur piangi"; "Mentre l'ardite labbia." In *Ghirlanda de madrigali for 4 voices* (1593), edited by Cees Wagemakers. Rijswijk, the Netherlands: Stichting Donemus Beheer, 2016.

• La Villanella Basel. *O Dulcis Amor*, 2004.

Casulana, Maddalena. "Io d'odorate fronde" from *Il secondo libro de madrigali*. Choral Public Domain Library. https://www.cpdl.org/wiki/index.php/Io_d%27odorate_(Maddalena_Casulana)

———. "Ridon' hor per le piagge" from *Il secondo libro de madrigali.* Choral Public Domain Library. https://www.cpdl.org/wiki/index.php/ Ridon%27_hor_per_le_piagge_(Maddalena_Casulana)

- Mädchenchor Hannover and Knabenchor Hannover. *Verklingend und ewig: Rarities from the Herzog August Bibliothek Wolfenbuttel,* 2013.

Sacred Vocal

Aleotti, Raffaella (also Vittoria). *Sacrae Cantiones: Quinque, Septem, Octo & Decem Vocibus Decantandae.* Edited by C. Ann Carruthers. New York: Broude Trust, 2006.

- Cappella Artemisia. *Raphaella Aleotti: Sacrae Cantiones,* 2009.

Assandra, Caterina. "Duo Seraphim" from *Motetti à dua & tre voci, op. 2.* In *Two Sacred Works for Three Treble Voices,* edited by Barbara Garvey Jackson. Fayetteville, AR: ClarNan Editions, 1990.

- Cappella Artemisia. *Rosa Mistica: Musiche nei monasteri femminili lombardi del '600,* 1999.

Bermúdez, Pedro. "Christus natus est nobis." In *Choral Music from Guatemala,* edited by Dieter Lehnhoff. Niedernhausen, Germany: Edition Kemel, 2008.

- La Sfera Armoniosa. *Senhora del Mundo: Early Music from Spain, Portugal & the New World,* 2000.

———. "Misa de bomba." In *Las misas de Pedro Bermúdez,* edited by Dieter Lehnhoff. Guatemala City: Universidad Rafael Landivar, Instituto de Musicologia, 2001.

- Ars Nova de Guatemala. *Misa de Bomba a 4.* YouTube. https://www. youtube.com/watch?v=RxOirZOhQ2o

Fernandes (or Fernandez), Gaspar. "Xicochi Conetzintle," edited by V. Chavarria. Choral Public Domain Library. https://www.cpdl.org/wiki/index. php/Xicochi_xicochi_(Gaspar_Fernandes)

- Capilla Virreinal de la Nueva España. *La Música de la Catedral de Oaxaca, México,* 2005.

Franco, Hernando (or Fernando). "Magnificat: Quinti Toni." In *The Franco Codex of the Cathedral of Mexico,* edited by Steven Barwick. Carbondale: Southern Illinois University Press, 1965.

- Cappella Cervantina. *Música Barroca Mexicana,* 1998.

———. "Salve Regina." In *A New-World Collection of Polyphony for Holy Week and the Salve Service: Guatemala City, Cathedral Archive, Music MS 4,* edited by Robert J. Snow. Chicago, IL: University of Chicago Press, 1996.

- The Queen's Six. *Journey to the New World: Hispanic Sacred Music from the Sixteenth and Seventeenth Centuries*, 2020.

Lusitano, Vicente. "Heu me Domine." Edited by Peter Gibeau. IMSLP. https://imslp.org/wiki/Heu_me_Domine_(Lusitano%2C_Vicente)

- Huelgas Ensemble. *Canções, Vilancicos e Motets Portugueses: séculos XVI–XVII*, 1994.

———. "Regina caeli laetare." Edited by Samuel Brannon. IMSLP. https://imslp.org/wiki/Regina_caeli_laetare_(Lusitano%2C_Vicente)

- Choir of St. Andrew & St. Paul. Live recording. YouTube. https://www.youtube.com/watch?v=aDjwDdvJXJw

Peñalosa, Francisco de. "Sancta mater istud agas." In *A New-World Collection of Polyphony for Holy Week and the Salve Service: Guatemala City, Cathedral Archive, Music MS 4*, edited by Robert J. Snow. Chicago, IL: University of Chicago Press, 1996.

- Odhecaton. *Un Libro de Horas de Isabel la Católica*, 2006.

Instrumental

Assandra, Caterina. "Ave verum corpus"; "Ego flos campi." In *Organ Music by Women Composers Before 1800*, edited by Calvert Johnson. Pullman, WA: Vivace Press, 1993.

- La Villanella Basel. *O Dulcis Amor*, 2004.

Selected Secondary Sources

Austern, Linda Phyllis. "'For Musicke Is the Handmaid of the Lord': Women, Psalms, and Domestic Music-Making in Early Modern England." In *Psalms in the Early Modern World*, edited by Linda Phyllis Austern, Kari Boyd McBride, and David L. Orvis, 77–114. Burlington, VT: Ashgate, 2011.

Bermúdez, Egberto. "Urban Musical Life in the European Colonies: Examples from Spanish America, 1530–1650." In *Music and Musicians in Renaissance Cities and Towns*, edited by Fiona Kisby, 167–80. Cambridge: Cambridge University Press, 2001.

Blackburn, Bonnie J. "Professional Women Singers in the Fifteenth Century: A Tale of Two Annas." In *The Cambridge History of Fifteenth-Century Music*, edited by Anna Maria Busse Berger and Jesse Rodin, 476–85. Cambridge: Cambridge University Press, 2015.

Bloechl, Olivia. "Music in the Early Colonial World." In *The Cambridge History of Sixteenth-Century Music*, edited by Iain Fenlon and Richard Wistreich, 128–75. Cambridge: Cambridge University Press, 2019.

Borgerding, Todd M., ed. *Gender, Sexuality, and Early Music.* New York: Routledge, 2002.

- Nina Treadwell, "'Simil combattimento fatto da Dame': The Musico-Theatrical Entertainments of Margherita Gonzaga's *balletto delle donne* and the Female Warrior in Ferrarese Cultural History," 27–40.
- Kelley Harness, "Chaste Warriors and Virgin Martyrs in Florentine Musical Spectacle," 73–121.
- Liane Curtis, "Christine de Pizan and 'Dueil Angoisseux,'" 265–82.

Coelho, Victor Anand. "Connecting Histories: Portuguese Music in Renaissance Goa." In *Goa and Portugal: Their Cultural Links*, edited by Charles J. Borges and Helmut Feldmann, 131–47. New Delhi: Concept Publishing, 1997.

Feldman, Martha and Bonnie Gordon, eds. *The Courtesan's Arts: Cross-Cultural Perspectives*. New York: Oxford University Press, 2006.

- Dawn De Rycke, "On Hearing the Courtesan in a Gift of Song: The Venetian Case of Gaspara Stampa," 124–32.
- Drew Edward Davies, "On Music Fit for a Courtesan: Representations of the Courtesan and Her Music in Sixteenth-Century Italy," 144–58.

Filippi, Daniele V. "Songs in Early Modern Catholic Missions: Between Europe, the Indies, and the 'Indies of Europe.'" *Troja: Jahrbuch für Renaissancemusik* 14 (2015): 39–68.

Harrán, Don. "Tradition and Innovation in Jewish Music of the Later Renaissance." *The Journal of Musicology* 7, no. 1 (1989): 107–30.

Kaufmann, Miranda. *Black Tudors: The Untold Story*. London: Oneworld Publications, 2017.

- Chapter 1, "John Blanke, the Trumpeter"

Klinck, Anne L. and Ann Marie Rasmussen, eds. *Medieval Woman's Song: Cross-Cultural Approaches*. Philadelphia: University of Pennsylvania Press, 2001.

- Anne L. Klinck, "Sappho and Her Daughters: Some Parallels Between Ancient and Medieval Woman's Song," 15–28.
- Susan Boynton, "Women's Performance of the Lyric Before 1500," 47–65.

Michelini, Ann N. "Women and Music in Ancient Greece and Rome." In *Women and Music: A History*, 2nd ed., edited by Karin Pendle, 21–25. Bloomington: Indiana University Press, 2001.

Monson, Craig A., ed. *The Crannied Wall: Women, Religion, and the Arts in Early Modern Europe*. Ann Arbor: University of Michigan Press, 1992.

- Carolyn Valone, "Roman Matrons as Patrons: Various Views of the Cloister Wall," 49–72.
- H. Colin Slim, "Music and Dancing with Mary Magdalen in a Laura Vestalis," 139–60.
- Patrick Macey, "*Infiamma il mio cor*: Savonarolan *Laude* by and for Dominican Nuns in Tuscany," 161–89.

O'Malley, John W., Gauvin Alexander Bailey, Steven J. Harris, and T. Frank Kennedy, eds. *The Jesuits: Cultures, Sciences, and the Arts, 1540–1773.* Toronto: University of Toronto Press, 1999.

- Paulo Castagna, "The Use of Music by the Jesuits in the Conversion of the Indigenous Peoples of Brazil," 641–58.
- William J. Summers, "The Jesuits in Manila, 1581–1621: The Role of Music in Rite, Ritual, and Spectacle," 659–79.

Ros-Fábregas, Emilio. "'Imagine all the People...': Polyphonic Flowers in the Hands and Voices of Indians in 16th-Century Mexico." *Early Music* 40, no. 2 (May 2012): 177–89.

Stevenson, Robert. "European Music in 16th-Century Guatemala." *The Musical Quarterly* 50, no. 3 (1964): 341–52.

———. "The First Black Published Composer." *Inter-American Music Review/ Revista Interamericana* 5, no. 1 (Fall 1982): 79–103. [Vicento Lusitano]

Stoessel, Jason. "Voice and Song in Early Encounters Between Latins, Mongols, and Persians, ca. 1250–ca. 1350." In *Studies on a Global History of Music: A Balzan Musicology Project*, edited by Reinhard Strohm, 83–113. London: Routledge, 2018.

Stras, Laurie. "The Performance of Polyphony in Early 16th-Century Italian Convents." *Early Music* 45, no. 2 (2017): 195–215.

Takao, Makoto Harris. "'In Their Own Way': Contrafactal Practices in Japanese Christian Communities during the 16th Century." *Early Music* 47, no. 2 (2019): 183–98.

Teichler, Yael Sela. "*My Ladye Nevells Booke*: Music, Patronage and Cultural Negotiation in Late Sixteenth-Century England." *Renaissance Studies* 26, no. 1 (2012): 88–111.

Thomas, Jennifer. "Marguerite of Austria, Katherine of Aragon, and London Royal 8 G. vii." In *Musical Voices of Early Modern Women: Many-Headed Melodies*, edited by Thomasin La May. 337–64. Burlington, VT: Ashgate, 2005.

Woodfield, Ian. "The Keyboard Recital in Oriental Diplomacy, 1520–1620." *Journal of the Royal Musical Association* 115, no. 1 (1990): 33–62.

Yardley, Anne Bagnall. "'Ful wel she soong the service dyvyne': The Cloistered Musician in the Middle Ages." In *Women Making Music: The Western Art Tradition, 1150–1950,* edited by Jane Bowers and Judith Tick. 15–38. Urbana: University of Illinois Press, 1986.

———. *Performing Piety: Musical Culture in Medieval English Nunneries.* New York: Palgrave Macmillan, 2006.

- Chapter 4, "Everyday Musical Practices: Psalters, Hours, and the Office of the Dead"
- Chapter 6, "The Consecration of Nuns"

2 Music between 1600 and 1750

Introduction

By 1600, Europeans had explored the world outside their continent for about a century. Spain, Portugal, France, and England were the primary colonizing nations, partnering with private companies that often wielded government-like powers over Indigenous populations in the areas they conquered. This resulted in new sources of wealth for many Europeans. Jesuits, Dominicans, and Franciscans established missions and churches throughout the world as part of the expanding Spanish and Portuguese Empires. Art music and European instruments often arrived in a new area with priests, nuns, and monks who used music to evangelize. By the early eighteenth century, some churches in larger urban areas and established missions had robust musical institutions with staffs that combined European-born with Indigenous and/or enslaved musicians.

Protestant groups also used music to evangelize and attempt to "westernize" native populations. For example, Moravian hymns from North America with texts in Mohican (some translated from German or English, others seemingly written by Mohicans) survive from the early eighteenth century.[1] Although native and enslaved people resisted as well as adapted to the imposition of European culture on them, surviving documentation often allows little more than theorizing from creative readings of documents written from the settlers' point of view to discern the Indigenous experience.

In areas conquered by Spain and Portugal, many Indigenous people were forced to leave their homes and move to settlements called *reducción* or *mission* (missions) which were founded to begin the process of mass conversions to Christianity by Jesuit missionaries and support imperial economic policies. The extreme regulation of monastic daily schedules imposed by Jesuit practice, combined with the music and

DOI: 10.4324/9781003044635-3

sounds present in Catholic ritual helped to impose European versions of "order" and "civility" on Indigenous populations.[2] Corporate worship in many missions relied on communal singing of simple plainchants and hymns from memory although practices varied by region.[3] European and locally-born composers in Mexico, Central, and South America wrote music with texts in local languages and must surely have heard music that originated in Indigenous and African cultures, even if documentation is often lacking to quantify the exact influence these traditions had on European-style religious and secular music.[4]

The interest and skill of one priest could support European musical activities for a time, but as soon as he left or died, the resources and skills to perform the repertoire quickly decayed or disappeared entirely in many areas. This limited the sophistication and complexity of the European music that musicians could perform in many colonized locations.[5] In Spanish-occupied Puerto Rico during the seventeenth century, for example, church leaders tried to ban or minimize African-derived religious practices such as dancing during services and public festivities in an attempt to suppress "an autonomous Christian-based syncretic vernacular religion."[6] However, the Puerto Rican diocese lacked the material resources (organs, prayer books, etc.) and personnel trained in Spanish Catholic music to implement these restrictions.[7] Instead, what Noel Allende-Goitía calls a "coculture" emerged that incorporated elements of African and local Indigenous religious practices with music from Spain, most notably in the *villancico*.[8] Recent research indicates that of the global Jesuit missions, those located along the border between the Spanish and Portuguese empires boasted the most stable musical institutions and the most abundant musical resources.[9]

While the church was the site of much of the music making in the colonies, some cities were able to support other cultural institutions as well. As Spanish-language opera became more popular in Spain, a transatlantic exchange ensued between the European continent and New Spain with operatic performances occurring first in Lima, then Mexico City, and eventually the Jesuit missions in South America. The first extant opera written in the Spanish colonies was *La púrpura rosa* by Tomás de Torrejón (1701), inspired by a 1660 play by Pedro Calderón de la Barca. It celebrated the new King of Spain, Philip V, and promoted the Peruvian viceroy's support of the French Bourbons over the Austrian Habsburgs in the War of Succession.[10]

Nuns in Europe and other parts of the world took on leadership positions in convents, participated in intellectual pursuits, and composed, performed, and published music. In Mexico, Sister Juana Inés de la Cruz (1651–95), called the Tenth Muse during her lifetime, was the most important public intellectual and literary figure in the Hispanic world of the late seventeenth century. A poet and essayist, she argued for women's right to an education and wrote about Catholic theology, science, music, and acoustics.[11] Religious houses were also robust cultural centers across Europe and in colonized areas. Music in the religious houses of Cuzco, for example, played a significant role in the cultural life of the Viceroyalty of Peru during the seventeenth century. Convents accepted novitiates from Spanish and Incan backgrounds but maintained an internal hierarchy that placed settlers above Indigenous women. Two prominent convents in Cuzco became so intimately connected to the local settler elite that the cultural activities in these houses became a source of civic pride and Hispanic identity. Convents around the world offered talented women musicians special perks to join their ranks, including a reduced or waived dowry and agreements that limited their duties outside of musical services.[12] Nuns who brought revenue to their convents often received stipends for their musical work and retained control of this money.[13] Especially skilled musicians could become famous in their locales, bringing prestige to themselves, their families of origin, and their convents. Nuns also composed music and in some cases were the leading composers in their areas, including Lucrezia Orsina Vizzana (early seventeenth-century Bologna), Chiara Margarita Cozzolani (mid-seventeenth-century Milan), and Maria Anna von Raschenau (early eighteenth-century Vienna).

Music was an important component of a wealthy woman's education. Some women became active patrons because of a love of music, a desire to shape their public personas through the arts, or as part of their familial duties. As was true in the Renaissance, women's courts offered unique opportunities for composers and musicians, although the music produced for women leaders sometimes supported different purposes than those required by their male counterparts. For example, when Maria Maddalena of Austria (1587–1631) was regent for her son Ferdinando II of Florence, she needed to establish her authority in a way that a man would not. The operas composed during her reign asserted a spiritual basis for women's claims to authority by dramatizing the lives of Biblical women whose power was derived from God.[14] Francesca Caccini wrote three of these works, among the very few operas commissioned from a woman composer during this period.

Women operatic performers could exert some influence over the roles they created. George Frideric Handel, for example, tailored the arias he wrote to the vocal strengths of the singers he worked with.[15] Some prima donnas became quite successful but were dependent for work on a network of impresarios who hired singers for the opera houses of Europe. While some women attained fame and fortune through their work on the stage, many other women played music in more private spaces. Courtesans often had musical skills and the vocal bravura required for elaborate melodic ornamentation was part of their mystique.[16]

Although their numbers were still relatively small, eighteenth-century German courts employed 380 Black court servants or "court Moors" as they were called at the time. Many were instrumentalists, with the majority working as pipers and drummers in the military. While their exact legal and social status is debated by scholars, these musicians were guild members who often married local German women and were viewed as a source of prestige for the courts where they worked.[17] Some enslaved Africans received Western musical training. There were even a few orchestras staffed by enslaved people in Batavia (now Jakarta), Macao, and a Dutch outpost in Nagasaki.[18]

Locales & Locations

Many European women spent their lives in convents because their families thought they would be safe from dishonor and their maintenance or marriage dowries would not drain resources from the family.[19] The Council of Trent decreed a strict enclosure of nuns in their houses in the late sixteenth century, limiting the women's contact with the outside world, though the extent to which these rules were followed varied. For instance, the nuns at a Benedictine convent called Nonnberg Abbey in Salzburg did not begin to comply with these orders until about 1620.[20] The mandates prohibited outside musicians from entering the convent, which prompted the nuns at Nonnberg to take on more musical duties themselves. The convent recruited women who already had musical training (such as Anna Maria Pfisterer, an organist and music teacher) and relatives of important musicians in the area (including Anna Magdalena, daughter of Heinrich Ignaz Franz Biber von Bibern). Nonnberg Abbey became famous for its music, facilitating a connection to the city as well as providing a much needed outlet for entertainment for nuns who had little contact with others.[21] While convents were often famous for polyphonic sacred music, nuns also performed instrumental music and staged theatrical productions although the stories were usually centered on Biblical figures or saints.[22] As the music in convents became more famous, however, their ceremonies and elaborate performances often sparked a backlash from church authorities who were afraid the nuns would disgrace the church or that the sumptuous festivities outweighed the religious goals of the worship service. For example, Bishop Giacomo Boncompagni prohibited the use of music in the convents of Bologna in 1703, although some houses ignored his order. Music was part of a campaign of resistance by nuns against Church control over their houses that periodically resurfaced throughout this era.[23]

Forms & Factions

The production and patronage of classical music depended upon the wealth of individuals and the support of governmental and church institutions. By the seventeenth century, much of that wealth in Britain, France, Spain, and Portugal was derived from the slave trade and enslaved labor. For instance, Handel benefitted personally from investments he made in slave trading companies as did his patrons. Handel periodically owned stock in the South Sea Company beginning in 1715 or 1716, and later bought a South Sea Annuity.[24] When the composer first acquired his stock, the South Sea Company had a right to forty-five percent of the profit generated from the trade of African people bound for enslavement in the Spanish colonies in the Americas.[25] Handel sold his stock in the South Sea Company in 1732 and used that money to help defray the costs of his opera seasons for the rest of the decade.[26] In 1720, the Duke of Chandos, one of Handel's patrons, along with men in his circle (including Handel himself) invested heavily in the Royal African Company, England's biggest slave-trading company. The investors in the company also helped finance London's musical life. One-third of the people who subscribed to the Royal Academy of Music during its existence between 1719 and 1727 also held stock in the Royal African Company. Handel was the musical director of the Royal Academy of Music and composed many of his Italian operas for the organization including *Giulio Cesare in Egitto,* the hit of the 1724–25 season. Many of Handel's manuscripts survive today because they were part of collections purchased by families whose wealth depended upon enslaved labor.[27]

Responses & Reception

Although art music circulated globally because of colonization, leaders also took advantage of classical music as part of cultural diplomacy. The diplomatic dance between the French court led by Louis XIV (ruled 1643–1715) and Siam and its ruler, Phra Narai (ruled 1656–88), featured musical encounters beginning in 1673 when the two rulers established diplomatic relations. Musicians and Jesuit missionaries were part of all French delegations to Siam from the first trip in 1685. These visitors brought European instruments and scores with them, which established a small presence of Western music in Siam.[28] Some of these visitors also wrote descriptions of the music they heard during their travels, which constitute some of the only extant accounts of Siamese music from the period.[29] Meanwhile, Siamese diplomats visiting France heard a great deal of music, including operas, ceremonial music, and sacred choral works. Misunderstandings between the two groups abounded, such as when two Siamese visitors stormed out of a performance of Lully's *Roland* because they interpreted their front row seats as an affront. Prestige in Siam was signaled by sitting in an elevated position over others. The French also clumsily tried to connect with Siamese delegations by performing exoticized Western art music for them with what the French thought of as "Asian" characteristics, but which contained no authentic musical references to Siam (or any other Asian musical tradition).[30] These early attempts at cultural diplomacy might have led to some difficult moments, but they also represent an example of engagement between a European and a non-European country on a more equal footing than the inequitable encounters between colonizer and colonized.[31]

Notes

1 Rachel Wheeler and Sarah Eyerly, "Singing Box 331: Re-sounding Eighteenth-Century Mohican Hymns from the Moravian Archives," *The William and Mary Quarterly* 76, no. 4 (October 2019): 649–96.

2 Guillermo Wilde, "Toward a Political Anthropology of Mission Sound: Paraguay in the 17th and 18th Centuries," trans. Eric Ederer, *Music & Politics* 1, no. 2 (Summer 2007): 9.

3 Kristin Dutcher Mann, *The Power of Song: Music and Dance in the Mission Communities of Northern New Spain, 1590–1810* (Stanford, CA: Stanford University Press, 2013), 103.

4 For one example of this phenomenon from Robert Stevenson's scholarship see Chapter 3 in *Music in Mexico: A Historical Survey* (New York: Thomas Y. Crowell Co., 1952).

5 Leonardo Waisman, "Music in the Jesuit Missions of the Upper Marañón," in *Cultural Worlds of the Jesuits in Colonial Latin America*, ed. Linda A. Newsom (London: University of London Press, 2020), 111–26, at 122.

6 Noel Allende-Goitía, "The Mulatta, the Bishop, and Dances in the Cathedral: Race, Music, and Power Relations in Seventeenth-Century Puerto Rico," *Black Music Research Journal* 26, no. 2 (Fall 2006): 137–64, at 146, 150.

7 Allende-Goitía, "Race, Music," 154.

8 Allende-Goitía, "Race, Music," 155–60. He notes that evidence for these types of creolized cultural practices exists throughout seventeenth-century Spanish-controlled areas.

9 The archives of colonial music at the Seminary of San Antonio Abad in Cuzco, Peru, has 400 works from this period, almost all *villancicos* and vesper psalms.

10 This paragraph is based on Chad M. Gasta, *Transatlantic Arias: Early Opera in Spain and the New World* (Frankfurt am Main: Vervuert, 2013), 11–31.

11 Enrique Alberto Arias, "Sor Juana Inés de la Cruz and Music: Mexico's 'Tenth Muse,'" in *Musical Voices of Early Modern Women: Many-Headed Melodies*, ed. Thomasin LaMay (London: Routledge, 2016), 311–34. Her musical treatise is no longer extant.

12 Geoffrey Baker, "Music in the Convents and Monasteries of Colonial Cuzco," *Latin American Music Review* 24, no. 1 (Spring–Summer 2003): 1–41, at 1–9. For a European example of women recruited to convents in Castile because of their musical talent see Colleen Baade, "'Hired' Nun Musicians in Early Modern Castile," in *Musical Voices of Early Modern Women: Many-Headed Melodies*, ed. Thomasin LaMay (London: Routledge, 2016), 287–310.

13 Baade, "'Hired' Nun Musicians," 294.

14 Kelley Harness, "Chaste Warriors and Virgin Martyrs in Florentine Musical Spectacle," in *Gender, Sexuality, and Early Music*, ed. Todd C. Borgerding (London: Routledge, 2002), 73–122, at 75.

15 Thomas Forrest Kelly, *First Nights at the Opera* (New Haven, CT: Yale University Press, 2004), 15.

16 Shawn Marie Keener, "Virtue, Illusion, *Venezianità:* Vocal Bravura and the Early *Cortigiana Onesta*," in *Musical Voices of Early Modern Women*, ed. Thomasin LaMay (London: Routledge, 2016), 119–34.

17 Arne Spohr, "'Mohr und Trompeter': Blackness and Social Status in Early Modern Germany," *Journal of the American Musicological Society* 72, no. 3 (2019): 613–63.

18 Margaret Kartomi, *Musical Journeys in Sumatra* (Urbana: University of Illinois Press, 2012), 241–42. These orchestras seemed to be employed mostly for background music and to accompanying dancing. Denis-Constant Martin, *Sounding the Cape: Music, Identity and Politics in South Africa* (Somerset West, South Africa: African Minds Publishers, 2013), 70.

19 In mid-seventeenth-century Siena, about twelve percent of the female population lived in a convent. Colleen Reardon, "The Good Mother, the Reluctant Daughter, and the Convent: A Case of Musical Persuasion," in *Musical Voices of Early Modern Women*, ed. Thomasin LaMay (London: Routledge, 2016), 271–86, at 273.

20 Barbara Lawatsch Melton, "Loss and Gain in a Salzburg Convent: Tridentine Reform, Princely Absolutism, and the Nuns of Nonnberg (1620 to 1696)," in *Enduring Loss in Early Modern Germany: Cross Disciplinary Perspectives*, ed. Lynne Tatlock (Boston: Brill, 2010), 259–80, at 259.

21 Melton, "Loss and Gain," 270–74.

22 Colleen Reardon, *Holy Concord within Sacred Walls: Nuns and Music in Siena, 1575–1700* (New York: Oxford University Press, 2001), Chapters 4 and 6.

23 Craig Monson, *Disembodied Voices: Music and Culture in an Early Modern Italian Convent* (Berkeley: University of California Press, 1995), 225–38.

24 Sources differ as to the year Handel first invested in the South Sea Company. For details, see Ellen T. Harris, "Handel the Investor," *Music & Letters* 85, no. 4 (November 2004): 521–75.

25 Rafael Donoso Anes, "Accounting and Slavery: The Accounts of the English South Sea Company, 1713–22," *The European Accounting Review* 11, no. 2 (2002): 441–52, at 442.

26 David Hunter, *The Lives of George Frideric Handel* (Woodbridge: Boydell Press, 2015), 200–7.

27 See David Hunter, "Handel Manuscripts and the Profits of Slavery: The 'Granville' Collection at the British Library and the First Performing Score of *Messiah* Reconsidered," *Notes* 76, no. 1 (September 2019): 27–37; and Hunter, "The Beckfords in England and Italy: A Case Study in the Musical Uses of the Profits of Slavery," *Early Music* 46, no. 2 (May 2018): 285–98.

28 Large-scale musical exchange between the West and Siam did not occur until the nineteenth century.

29 Archival resources from this period in Siam were largely destroyed in 1767. Surviving documents are primarily written from the French perspective, which reveal curiosity about Siamese music colored by a dismissive attitude influenced by exoticized stereotypes that French observers believed about Asian people.

30 *Roland,* for example, includes an orientalist representation of China.

31 This paragraph is based on David R. M. Irving, "Lully in Siam: Music and Diplomacy in French-Siamese Cultural Exchanges, 1680–1690," *Early Music* 40, no. 3 (2012): 393–420.

Lesson 2.1: Manuel de Sumaya, *Miserere*

Background

Mexican composer and organist Manuel de Sumaya [Zumaya] (c. 1678–1755) is among the "most remarkable New World composers of the 18th century" because of his dexterous handling of late-Renaissance vocal polyphonic styles as well as his use of instruments in cathedral music.[1] He was one of the few Baroque-era musicians born and educated in colonial Latin America. The church (and the music of the church) was central to his life.[2] Sumaya was trained at an early age by the resident chapel master and principal organist in Mexico City, learning counterpoint and liturgy and ultimately assumed the chapel master position in 1715. Before becoming chapel master, he showed much promise as a student of contrapuntal styles, and he is also known for composing the music for *La Parténope* (1711), the first opera written by a North American-born composer.[3] Although Sumaya composed many Latin-texted liturgical works following what colonizers deemed "models suitable for Christian worship," he also composed sacred works set in Spanish called *villancicos*, which borrowed from a "more secular Hispanic tradition while generally maintaining the sacred music idiom of the period."[4] His contributions to the musical life of Mexico City were not limited to composing music for services, as he also taught students and supervised the copying of choir books. He was one of the most innovative compositional voices in cathedral music during his time, as he is credited with expanding the breadth and function of the orchestra by hiring additional strings, brass, and winds during his tenure as chapel master in Mexico City.[5] Sumaya left Mexico City for Oaxaca in 1738 and served in liturgical, educational, and musical capacities there until his death in 1755. He was a prolific composer of church music, whose works include a number of Masses, *villancicos*, psalm settings, Lamentations, and Misereres.

Miserere (1717)

Sumaya's *Miserere* is a "four-voiced setting of the odd numbered verses and the second half of verse 20 of Psalm 50 ... Sung at Lauds in Holy Week, Psalm 50 was also used in the Office for the Dead and for burial service."[6] It is to be performed "alternatim," which means the alternating even numbered verses are sung as plainchant. The text and translation for the excerpt follow:[7]

1. Miserere mei, Deus, secundum magnam misericordiam tuam.
   Have mercy upon me, O God, according to your great mercy.
3. Amplius lava me ab iniquitate mea: et a peccato meo munda me.
   Wash me thoroughly from my iniquity, and cleanse me from my sin.
5. Tibi soli peccavi, et malum coram te feci: ut justificeris in sermonibus tuis, et vincas cum judicaris.
   Against you only have I sinned, and have done evil in your sight. And, so you are justified when you speak and upright in your judgment.
7. Ecce enim veritatem dilexisti: incerta et occulta sapientiae tuae manifestasti mihi.
   For behold, you look for truth deep within me, and will make me understand wisdom secretly.

Barwick refers to the setting as a "simple chordal style," and the prevailing homophonic texture supports that reading. There are also moments of light polyphony that activate the texture at key moments in the text and provide momentum through phrases. The setting is, indeed, simple when compared to some of the imitative writing and polychoral treatments in the *villancicos*. The following commentary is based primarily on the Barwick transcription—the odd numbered verses of the Psalm. As the intervening verses of plainchant interrupt the common meter, Barwick's numbering of measures and placement of double bars coincide with the beginnings and endings of verses.

Thus, each verse begins with measure 1, and references to system numbers will aid in locating our points of emphasis and reference.

This music is mostly diatonic, and each verse in this excerpt begins on an F major triad. Sumaya also takes several jaunts that briefly visit harmonic areas such as D minor and C major. This is facilitated through the use of accidentals, or *musica ficta*. Barwick noted that instances of the practices/occurrences of *musica ficta* are designated above the staff while accidentals that appear next to the note were written that way in the manuscript.[8] Whereas the F is established in the opening measures, Sumaya briefly visits D minor and C major in the first verse. While neither should be thought of as "modulations," they both show the flexibility of modes through the incorporation of accidentals, the relative strength of the bass movement by fifth (mm. 3–4 and 5–6; system 2), and points of relative rhythmic repose. Indeed, the plea for God's mercy moves to D minor while the hope within God's goodness propels us back toward F with a brief resolution to C ("secundum magnam") and a slight shift to an imitative texture. Note also the 4–3 suspensions between the bass and soprano in measure 3 (beats 3 and 4) and the bass and tenor in measure 9 (beats 1 and 2) at cadential points. "Consonant fourth" suspensions occur throughout the piece as well and are, at times, favored at cadences (see also system 7, m. 13; system 8, m. 3; system 9, m. 5).[9]

Verse 3, beginning in system 4, signals an even more specific petition, as the psalmist asks to be cleansed from sin and guilt. The *ficta* in the opening measures of this verse aids in negating awkward augmented second leaps in the soprano's ascent toward D. This petition hints toward D minor before resting on an F chord in measure 5, and the evoking of iniquity and guilt draw us back to the D minor sonority in measure 8. Before polyphony interrupts the mostly homorhythmic texture of this verse, E♭ is introduced in the bass voice in m. 10. The E♭ was introduced to avoid the tritone leap in the bass voice. The E♭ in the bass moves downward by step to D and all other voices at that moment move stepwise to a member of a D minor triad, yielding an interesting M6–octave resolution where the bass moves by half step—a "Phrygian motion" that sometimes accompanies texts of a somber or sorrowful nature.[10] This added feature within the local minor modal context of sin heightens the effect of the psalmist's petition, as the verse ends on C (half cadence) with a decorated 4–3 suspension.

The complexity of the psalmist's confession is realized in Sumaya's treatments of verse 5 (system 8). Whereas the "chordal style" remains prevalent up to this point, the more notable shifts toward imitative textures at moments when second-person pronouns are prominent.

One instance of such a shift occurred near the conclusion of verse 1 (mm. 6–8) with the text, "misericordiam tuam" or "your kindness." Three second-person pronouns are given in the translation of verse 5, and Sumaya utilizes similar imitative treatments at moments that coincide with second-person positions. Sumaya sets the text "ut justificeris sermonibus tuis" (m. 9, system 10) with imitative treatments between the inner and outer voices. While the statement of F# in measure 11 creates interesting cross relations with the F-naturals, locally, it also highlights the progression to the G sonority at the end of the measure, offering additional color to a plagal arrival, of sorts, on D minor in the following measure. The imitation continues through a slight overlap in phrasing with the alto, as the next arrival on the C chord signals the end of the imitative episode. Perhaps, the two layers of musical activity at these moments suggest a fractured vulnerability within the confessional posture. Verse 5 concludes with a 7–6 suspension (bass/alto, m. 18, system 12) that is part of a diminished 6/3 triad that prepares the cadence on C that also initiates repeated, terraced entrances of "cum judicaris" before landing on a half cadence in D minor.

Sumaya emphasizes Bb in the bass at the beginning of verse 7 (system 13), when the psalmist acknowledges God's pleasure with "sincerity of heart." Visits to D minor and C major occur expectedly, with suspensions aiding in preparing those arrivals in measures 4–5 and 7–8, respectively. Sumaya propels the passage toward its cadence with a florid polyphonic episode, marked with layered statements of the text, "manifestasti mihi," and strings of running eighth notes in the outer voices. The increased rhythmic and affective charge is intensified by the incorporation of the Eb in measure 16. This colorful pitch averts the potential augmented fourth with the bass and aids in affirming the progression to the cadential-defining Bb triad, as the plagal cadence on F provides veritable closure to this sacred and searching text.

Locales & Locations

Drew Edward Davies states that Sumaya's "broad significance to music history" is in part due to his "seem[ing] to have been the first New Spanish composer to systematically write music for violins as a constituent part of cathedral ensembles, thus contributing to the diversification of musical practices in New Spanish churches."[11] Noting the "progressive" incorporation of violins in cathedral practice beginning around the 1710s, Davies documents Sumaya's hiring of violinists between 1715 and 1720 as well as "increasingly idiomatic" writing for the violin around that same time. Bearing in mind the relative proximity of these developments to the production of the opera attributed to Sumaya (*La Parténope*), the timing and considerations of potential influences are compelling. Barwick speculates that Sumaya might have lived in Italy because the composer could speak Italian and had access to the libretto.[12] Scholars have documented the Spanish viceroy's penchant for Italian opera and he was pleased with Sumaya's *La Parténope*, so one might assume that, along with elements of an Italian style, the composer may have also gleaned inspirations for expanding instrumental performance forces in cathedral music by way of his work on the opera.[13] Currently, there is no documentation of Sumaya living abroad and the majority of his works show a firm allegiance to traditional contrapuntal styles.

Further Consideration: From where did Sumaya's inspiration for greater incorporations of stringed instruments come? Could a residency in Italy, tied to his priesthood in New Spain, have even been possible? Consider all the music styles and genres to which he would have been exposed in conjunction with his talent. Potential inspirations notwithstanding, consider also the cultural and economic impact of the Cathedral hiring more musicians during Sumaya's tenure as chapel master. If most of the musicians were born and trained in Mexico, can we speculate about the confluence of styles and interpretative practices that would have resulted in forms such as the *villancico*?

Forms & Factions

There was likely some mixing of musical styles at mission sites in colonial Latin America, as one can assume that missionaries encountered the folk styles and dance music of the Indigenous people. However, "the European musical idioms were considered the only models suitable for Christian worship, [and] the church music of the Baroque period in Latin America exhibits little native stylistic orientation."[14] Despite this prevailing attitude among colonizers and European church leadership, genres such as "*villancicos* ... often set to texts in Indigenous languages or local dialects, incorporate[d] elements related to a more secular Hispanic tradition while generally maintaining the sacred idiom of the period."[15] Sumaya's *villancicos* were well-received.[16] They were composed for special events such as the feasts of Christmas, the Virgin of Guadalupe, and the Immaculate Conception of Mary. These works, in Spanish, feature adventurous choral writing (polychoral settings) and idiomatic writing for violins as well an increased complexity in style (such as more sequences in the bass lines).[17] Indeed, Sumaya demonstrated a firm grasp of the European polyphonic traditions, but his versatility and move toward modern Baroque styles are illustrated in the folk-inspired *villancicos*.

Further Consideration: Behague states that *villancicos* and similar pieces resonated well in Spanish churches in the early seventeenth century and in Mexican churches.[18] Why might this have been? Although missions and colonial church leadership promoted European musical styles as "suitable" for worship, sonic connections to vernacular culture in religious services were likely agents in fortifying a sense community.

Responses & Reception

As Sumaya ascended through the ranks of musicians in the Mexico City Cathedral, he was afforded many privileges such as access to Italian libretti and opportunities to study with higher ranking musicians. Antonio de Salazar, Sumaya's predecessor as chapel master, was one of those musicians. As Salazar's tenure came to an end, a small rivalry may have developed between Sumaya and an older musical associate in the Cathedral, Francisco de Atienza, who protested Sumaya's promotion as assistant to Salazar in 1710.[19] Craig Russell suggests that the older Atienza may have felt slighted by being "skipped over in preference for a 'mere' choirboy" and offers an account of the selection process for the position of chapel master in 1715:

> The two competed against each other for several days in exams that probed their abilities, knowledge, and expertise in nearly every area of music ... on June 3—in one of the most demanding trials—each applicant was presented with a *villancico* text and asked to set it to music. This was a standard exam of the time ... Sumaya dashed off the jaunty and imaginative *Sol-fa de Pedro* for four voices and continuo and summarily was acclaimed the victor on June 7.[20]

Atienza left Mexico City to fill a vacant chapel master position in Puebla, and Sumaya continued to thrive in the musical life of the Cathedral for the next two decades.[21]

Further Consideration: Considering the battery of tests for the juried competition between Sumaya and Atienza, can we speculate about the particular significance of the *villancico*? Since *villancicos* were set apart from the traditional liturgical music in the Cathedral, placing the folk-oriented form in such a weighted position suggests that leadership in the Mexico City Cathedral offered space for aspirants' creativity and valued the cultural significance of sacred music in the language of its parishioners.

Miserere (1717)

Manuel de Sumaya

14

Notes

1 Craig H. Russell, "Zumaya [Sumaya], Manuel de, *Grove Music Online.*

2 Drew Edward Davies, ed., *Manuel de Sumaya: Villancicos from Mexico City* (Middleton, WI: A-R Editions, 2019), xii.

3 Gerard Béhague, "Music in the 'New World': The Baroque in Mexico and Brazil," in *The World of Baroque Music: New Perspectives*, ed. George B. Stauffer (Bloomington: Indiana University Press, 2006), 253–80, at 261.

4 Béhague, "Music in the 'New World,'" 256.

5 Craig H. Russell, "Manuel de Sumaya: Reexamining the *a Cappella* Choral Music of a Mexican Master," in *Encomium Musicae: Essays in Memory of Robert J. Snow*, ed. David Crawford (Hillsdale, NY: Pendragon Press, 2002), 91–106, at 94.

6 Steven Barwick, *Two Mexico City Choirbooks of 1717: An Anthology of Sacred Polyphony from the Cathedral of Mexico* (Carbondale: Southern Illinois University Press, 1982), xxx–xxxi.

7 Barwick, *Two Mexico City Choirbooks*, xxxi. The musical example and text are transcribed from the score as rendered in Barwick's volume. The score does not include the even verse plainchant, but the recording used for this study incorporates the plainchant. Hence, only odd numbered verses are given in the text to coincide with the score. The translation is borrowed from the *Psalter: The Online Book of Common Prayer.* (https://www.bcponline.org/Psalter/the_psalter.html#51).

8 Barwick, *Two Mexico City Choirbooks*, xxvii. Notes that appear in parenthesis above the staff are Barwick's "own" suggestions for *musica ficta*, as he "tried to apply the rules of mi contra fa and subsemionium modi as well as practices that might seem to be indicated by added directives found in the manuscripts themselves." It should also be noted that accidentals would be added by the singers themselves, as they were expected to be aware of contrapuntal procedures and adjustments that needed to occur in real time during performance.

9 In this type of suspension, "the fourth ... falls on a weak beat, is approached by step (usually from above), and is followed immediately by a 4-3 suspension over the dominant note in the lowest voice." Thomas Benjamin, *The Craft of Modal Counterpoint: A Practical Approach* (New York: Routledge Press, 2005), 98.

10 Timothy R. McKinney, *Adrian Willaert and the Theory of Interval Affect: The Musica Nova Madrigals and the Novel Theories of Zarlino and Vicentino* (Burlington, VT: Ashgate Publishing, 2010), 102. Although McKinney discusses this motion in music of the sixteenth century, the somber affect in Sumaya's usage is notable and comparable to that of composers from preceding eras.

11 Davies, *Manuel de Sumaya*, xiii.

12 Barwick, *Two Mexico City Choirbooks*, xiii.

13 Barwick, *Two Mexico City Choirbooks*, xxii. See also Davies, *Manuel de Sumaya*, xv.

14 Béhague, "Music in the 'New World,'" 255–56.

15 Béhague, "Music in the 'New World,'" 255–56.

16 Davies, *Manuel de Sumaya*, ix.

17 Davies, *Manuel de Sumaya*, xiii.

18 Béhague, "Music in the 'New World,'" 256.
19 Russell, "Manuel de Sumaya," 92.
20 Russell, "Manuel de Sumaya," 92.
21 Barwick, *Two Mexico City Choirbooks*, xxii.

Lesson 2.2: The Network of Women around J. S. Bach

Background

One of the most persistent myths about classical music composers is that the best of them are solitary geniuses. This attitude has profoundly influenced scholarly study and teaching about classical music, which can devolve into a procession of "great men" and their music divorced from a larger context and the networks in which they moved. This lesson highlights some of the women that have been overlooked and marginalized in studies of Johann Sebastian Bach's music and career.

Johann's second wife, Anna Magdalena Wilcke, arrived in Cöthen in 1721 to be a court singer. Like most women in the era, Anna's musical training came from family members, as formal musical education was rarely available to women. Her salary of 300 talers was twice the amount paid to anyone else in the court musical establishment except for her future husband who made 100 talers more.[1] When she married Johann just five months after beginning her employment, their combined salary of 700 talers represented a third of the Prince of Cöthen's music budget. While at Cöthen, Johann wrote *Durchlauchtster Leopold*, a secular cantata praising their employer, which includes two bravura soprano arias doubtless intended for Anna to perform. When the family moved to Leipzig, Anna gave up her salaried position to care for their growing family, but she continued to make appearances in Cöthen and Weisenfels throughout the 1720s and seems to have helped in her children's musical education.[2]

Scholars have typically used Anna Magdalena's Notebooks to determine the chronology of Johann's compositions, rather than as a record of the family taste in music and Anna's skill as a performer and arranger. However, the 1725 book contains information about both these topics. For example, around 1731 Anna copied "Schlummert ein, ihr matten Augen" from her husband's cantata *Ich habe genug* into her Notebook, arranging it without the string parts and transposed up a third, presumably to fit her voice and the circumstances of home performance. Carl Phillipp Emanuel Bach wrote some of his earliest compositions in the book alongside copies of light dances and difficult keyboard pieces by other composers in multiple handwriting styles, suggesting that many people in the house were involved in music making. The dances are similar to those in keyboard collections marketed to the same kind of middle-class household maintained by the Bachs, indicating the family enjoyed the latest popular fare.[3] Sometimes, as Yo Tomita observes, Anna's and Johann's handwriting are "intertwined [in a manuscript] in such a manner that they must surely have discussed something about the copies they were making together."[4] We can only speculate on the influence Anna might have had on some of Johann's compositional decisions. David Yearsley argues that many of the pieces in the 1725 Notebook reflect Lutheran ideology about death and mourning, concluding that the pieces were part of Anna's (and perhaps her families') response to the premature deaths of seven of her children. Anna also copied a "raucous nuptial poem" at the end of the book that jokes about sex—subverting the popular image of Bach's stuffy moral rectitude.[5]

Christiane Mariane von Ziegler (1695–1760) was also an important woman in Johann Sebastian Bach's life. She hosted a Leipzig salon, was a significant literary figure (she wrote articles about German literature, and published two well-received books of poetry), and was the poet laureate at the University of Wittenberg. During Bach's lifetime, Ziegler was more celebrated than the composer in German-speaking lands.[6] In addition to her literary achievements, Ziegler was a musician, and she supplied the texts for nine of the works in Bach's second cycle of sacred cantatas.[7] No one knows how Bach met Ziegler, but he could have attended and even performed at her salon. Modeled after contemporary French salons, Ziegler's regular gathering was an important part of Leipzig's cultural landscape; a place where collaborators could connect and where she and other women could take part in artistic pursuits, as Leipzig laws and customs allowed few opportunities for women to perform in public venues.[8] Ziegler published the texts Bach used three years after the cantatas' composition. There are minor word changes and some omitted lines between the published versions and those that Bach used. Musicologists have claimed that Bach made changes to remedy weaknesses in Ziegler's texts. This thinking reflects a bias toward centering Bach as a genius who corrected the deficiencies in other people's work, particularly that of a woman. As George Stauffer notes, it is not clear that the libretto texts are superior to the published poems, and the differences between the two are similar to the minor alterations that Bach routinely made to the texts of his vocal music, which scholars do not use to deride the poet's skill when the writers are men.[9] Additionally, there is no reason to assume that Bach made the changes in the cantata texts on his own. It is just as likely that Ziegler made changes in the texts when she revised them for publication or that she and Bach collaborated to adapt her work for musical performance.[10]

Assumptions about Bach's superior skill, as well as limited views about women's roles in Leipzig, have contributed to women's erasure in Bach's biography. Most scholars have assumed that the Coffee Cantata premiered at Gottfried Zimmerman's coffee house with the soprano solos taken by a falsettist because of Leipzig's regulations prohibiting women from performing in public. A careful reading of the available documentation shows that, in fact, women performed at coffee houses in the city and that the regulations against female performers were directed at other kinds of businesses.[11] Katherine Goodman raises the possibility that the Coffee Cantata may have premiered at Ziegler's salon (a logical place for such a composition to be performed).[12] It is also possible that Ziegler wrote the text for the final two numbers in the cantata when Ließgen (the main character) outwits her father, whom she had been adroitly manipulating by pretending to agree with his plans to find her a husband. These verses are in keeping with Ziegler's feminist ideas as she argued that if women had the same opportunities, they could be the intellectual equals of men. David Yearsley even speculates that Bach's eldest daughter, Catharina Dorothea, may have sung the lead role in the cantata.[13]

Finally, musicologists have not fully explored Bach's connections to performers and composers throughout the German-speaking lands. Faustina Bordoni, for instance, was one of the most celebrated mezzo-sopranos of her era, and wife to Dresden-based composer Johann Adolf Hasse.[14] Scholars have long known that Bach traveled to Dresden, with his visits to Hasse often coinciding with Bordoni's important performances at the Dresden Opera House. Bordoni and her husband visited Leipzig several times, perhaps during the popular trade fairs that occurred three times per year. Thousands of visitors descended upon Leipzig to attend the fairs, and composers routinely sold printed editions of their work at the events.

Although no document has survived which confirms that Bach and Bordoni performed together, he conducted the *Missa* of his Mass in B minor (apparently angling for a court composer appointment) during a visit to Dresden in 1733. Arthur Mendel has suggested that the "Laudamus te" from the Gloria looks tailor-made for Bordoni's vocal strengths. In Leipzig, musicians worked overtime to entertain trade-fair visitors; Bach gave organ recitals and conducted the *collegium musicum* which presented extra concerts with visiting musicians as guest soloists.[15] It is certainly possible that Bordoni performed Bach's Italian cantata *Non sa che sia dolore* (BWV 209), which sits in her range, and/or one of the Italian-language pieces in the *collegium's* repertoire that were not by Bach when she was in Leipzig. George Stauffer writes that Bach seems to have quickly made parts for an early Italian cantata by Handel (*Dietro l'orme fuggaci*) for one concert during a trade fair which opens with an aria that features the kind of intricate ornamentation Bordoni was famous for.[16]

Locales & Locations

Scholars have examined Leipzig's musical landscape, but they primarily focus on the fields in which Bach was an active participant—music education, the Lutheran church, and the *collegium musicum*. This emphasis ignores the complete cultural landscape in Leipzig and creates the questionable impression that Bach would have been interested in, and only heard music in, a few physical locations and musical genres, and that all of Leipzig's musical entertainment was connected to Bach in some way. Recent research by Manuel Bärwald, for example, reveals that the Mingotti Italian opera troupe regularly visited Leipzig during the trade fairs between 1744 and 1756. They performed at least twenty different operas and intermezzi. None of the operas are in the current performing repertory, although Bärwald has located many of the libretti in libraries across Europe. Sometimes the singers in Mingotti's troupe performed as soloists with one of Leipzig's orchestras. His research indicates not only that Leipzig residents had regular and consistent access to Italian opera, but also that the repertoire they heard was quite different than the operas we prize from that period.[17]

Further Consideration: Ask students how they imagine Bach functioned as a musician in Leipzig. Did he have equally skilled colleagues? What musical institutions might have existed in the town besides those led by Bach? Help them consider why our image of canonical composers divorce them from wider networks of music making and musicians. Following this discussion, ask students how their conception of Bach and Leipzig is changed by understanding more about the cultural landscape in the area.

Forms & Factions

The information related here is more speculative than might usually be included in a lesson plan. The ambiguity about what we know of the relationships between Bach and the women in this essay reflects their absence from the archive and the shortcomings of musicological research. In some cases, the kind of documents that could provide evidence about the women in Bach's network were never created. (Bach did not need to write letters to his wife, for example, which means we know little about their working relationship.) Other documents were never saved, have been lost, and/or were overlooked by scholars interested in Bach at the expense of everyone else in his circle. A pervasive myth that most women and their activities are less important than men's means that the documentary evidence of their lives are less likely to be saved by their families and archives. The nineteenth-century biographers that might have had access to information now lost to us were invested in shaping an image of the composer that conformed to their ideas about the solitary genius, thus they suppressed, or at least ignored, evidence that could help us understand Bach's milieu more fully. This attitude spread to more recent historians who tend to interpret evidence in ways that center Bach's imagined point of view, as well as minimizing and even stigmatizing his interactions with other people, especially women. The tantalizing clues that Bach's life, career, and music were shaped by women in ways we are only beginning to understand may become clearer with more research, but without complete documentation we may never know the full story.

<u>Further Consideration:</u> Ask students to list all the documents that might help a future historian understand their lives and our time. Work with them to imagine how many of these documents might be saved for future researchers to find. Discuss how people in the future might understand the present based upon the documents they think scholars would have access to. What might they get wrong? What might they get right?

Responses & Reception

Anna Magdalena Bach has long been an object of popular curiosity. Beginning in the nineteenth century, several romanticized "biographies" and works of fiction about her were published. She is portrayed in these works as a dedicated wife who worshipfully devoted her life to her husband, only to die penniless and alone in 1760, ten years after her husband's passing. The partners of many famous composers have been similarly mythologized—Constanze Mozart as a spendthrift shrew; Clara Schumann as the grieving widow forced to return to a concert career to care for her eight children; and Cosima Wagner as the seductress who became Richard's loyal wife. In each case, these myths obscure the complexity of the lives and true accomplish-ments of these women. Their individuality has been sacrificed to fur-ther the legends about their husbands. Recently scholars have begun taking Anna Magdalena (and other composers' wives) seriously as a topic of study rather than assuming that the received wisdom is true. Yo Tomita and David Yearsley, among others, have started the pro-cess of separating the myths from the historical record and treating Anna as an important figure in her own right.[18] However, the collec-tive memory about Anna, and the other women mentioned in this paragraph, is powerful. It will take a concerted effort among musicol-ogists and teachers to correct the record and provide the public with a more accurate representation of Bach and the women in his life.

Further Consideration: Discuss the stereotypes around the concept of genius with students. Point out that "geniuses" are typically coded male and white.[19] How does this myth affect how classical music is studied by scholars, marketed to consumers, and audience's attitudes to the fine arts?

Notes

1 To avoid confusion, I will refer to the Bach family members by their first names when necessary. There is some disagreement in secondary sources as to Anna's salary. She may have earned 200 talers which would still make her the third highest-paid musician in the Cöthen court. See Andrew Talle, "Who was Anna Magdalena Bach?" *Bach* 51, no. 1 (2020): 139–71, 173, at 141.

2 This paragraph is based on David Yearsley, "Hoopskirts, Coffee, and the Changing Musical Prospects of the Bach Women," *Women & Music* 17 (2013): 27–58.

3 David Yearsley, "Death Everyday: The *Anna Magdalena Bach Book of 1725* and the Art of Dying," *Eighteenth-Century Music* 2, no. 2 (2005): 231–49, at 233.

4 Yo Tomita, "Anna Magdalena as Bach's Copyist," *Understanding Bach* 2 (2007): 59–76, at 60.

5 This poem is often suppressed in modern editions of the Notebook. David Yearsley, *Sex, Death, and Minuets: Anna Magdalena Bach and her Musical Notebooks* (Chicago, IL: University of Chicago Press, 2019), 43.

6 George B. Stauffer, "Women's Voices in Bach's Musical World: Christiane Mariane von Ziegler and Faustina Bordoni," in *Sara Levy's World: Gen-der, Judaism, and the Bach Tradition in Enlightenment Berlin*, ed. Rebecca Cypess and Nancy Sinkoff (Rochester, NY: University of Rochester Press, 2018), 75–96, at 77.

7 The cantatas with Ziegler texts are numbers 68, 74, 87, 103, 128, 175, 176, 183, and 187.

8 Mark A. Peters, *A Woman's Voice in Baroque Music: Mariane von Ziegler and J.S. Bach* (Burlington, VT: Ashgate, 2008), 42–45.

9 Stauffer, "Women's Voices," 80–83.
10 Stauffer, "Women's Voices," 81–82.
11 Yearsley, "Hoopskirts," 45.
12 Katherine R. Goodman, "From Salon to *Kaffeekranz*: Gender Wars and the *Coffee Cantata* in Bach's Leipzig," in *Bach's Changing World: Voices in the Community*, ed. Carol K. Baron (Rochester, NY: University of Rochester Press, 2006), 190–218.
13 Yearsley, "Hoopskirts."
14 Today Bordoni is famous because she starred in many of Handel's Italian operas and for her supposed rivalry with Francesca Cuzzoni. Recent scholarship shows this feud was a fiction sparked by satiric pamphlets and astute marketing. Even so, Suzanne Aspden argues that the intense coverage of the two prima donnas' relationship may have affected Handel's compositional approach to the operas they sang together. See Suzanne Aspden, *The Rival Sirens: Performance and Identity on Handel's Operatic Stage* (Cambridge: Cambridge University Press, 2013).
15 The records of performances in Leipzig during this period are incomplete.
16 This paragraph is based on Stauffer, "Women's Voices."
17 This paragraph is based on Manuel Bärwald, "Italian Opera Performances in Bach's Leipzig—New Sources and Perspectives on Research," *Understanding Bach* 6 (2011): 9–17.
18 Tomita, "Anna Magdalena as Bach's Copyist"; David Yearsley, "Death Everyday."
19 For a student-friendly blog post about this concept see Evan Williams, "The Myth of the Composer-Genius," *I Care If You Listen*, March 27, 2019, https://icareifyoulisten.com/2019/03/the-myth-of-the-composer-genius/.

Bibliography

Score/Recording

Opera

Torrejón, Tomás de. *La púrpura de la rosa*. Edited by Robert Stevenson. Lima: Instituto Nacional de Cultura, 1976.

- Ensemble Elyma. *La púrpura de la rosa*, 2000.

Secular Vocal

Bembo, Antonia. *Amor Mio*. Edited by Claire Fontijn. Bryn Mawr, PA: Hildegard Publishing Company, 1998.

- Armonia delle Sfere. *Bembo: Produzioni armoniche*, 2019.

Caccini, Settimia. *Four Arias*. Edited by Candace Smith. Bryn Mawr, PA: Hildegard Publishing, 1996.

- Ensemble Laus Concentus. *I Canti di Euterpe*, 1998.

Campana, Francesca. "Semplicetto augellin che mentre canti"; "S'io ti guardo ti sdegni"; "Occhi belli, occhi amati." In *Women Composers: Music Through the Ages, Vol. 2*, edited by Sylvia Glickman and Martha Furman Schleifer. New York: G. K. Hall & Co., 1996.

• Ensemble Ricercare Antico. *Campana: Arie a una, due e tre voci*, 2021.

Orsini, Eleonora (or Leonora). "Per pianto la mia carne." In *Women Composers: Music Through the Ages, Vol. 1*, edited by Sylvia Glickman and Martha Furman Schleifer. New York: G. K. Hall & Co., 1996.

• Ensemble Laus Concentus. *I Canti di Euterpe*. La Bottega Discantica, 1998.

Quinciani, Lucia. "Udite lagrimosi spirti." In *Women Composers: Music Through the Ages, Vol. 1*, edited by Sylvia Glickman and Martha Furman Schleifer. New York: G. K. Hall & Co., 1996.

• Ensemble Laus Concentus. *I Canti di Euterpe*. La Bottega Discantica, 1998.

Sacred Vocal

Badalla, Rosa Giacinta. "Non plangete." In *Celestial Sirens: Nuns and Their Music in Early Modern Milan*, edited by Robert L. Kendrick, 522–29. New York: Oxford University Press, 1996.

• *Earthly Angels: Music from 17th Century Nun Convents*, 2019.

Bembo, Antonia. *Tota pulchra es*. Edited by Claire Fontijn. Bryn Mawr, PA: Hildegard Publishing Company, 1998.

• Armonia delle Sfere. *Bembo: Produzioni armoniche*, 2019.

Billoni, Santiago. "Lauda Jerusalem." In *Santiago Billoni: Complete Works*, edited by Drew Edward Davies. Middleton, WI: A-R Editions, 2011.

• Austin Baroque Orchestra & Chorus. *Hecho en México (Live at Mission Concepción)*, 2020.

Cozzolani, Chiara Margarita. "Laudate pueri a 8." In *Salmi a otto voci concertati*, edited by Candace Smith and Bruce Dickey. Bologna, Italy: Artemisia Editions, 1999.

• Cappella Artemisia. *Cozzolani: I Vespri Natalizi*, 2012.

———. "O Coelu cives." In *Motets*, edited by Robert L. Kendrick. Middleton, WI: A-R Editions, 1998.

• Magnificat Baroque Ensemble. *Chiara Margarita Cozzolani: Complete Works, Vol. 1*, 2010.

Gutiérrez de Padilla, Juan. "Las estreyas se rien: juego de cañas a 3, y a 6." In *Latin American Colonial Music Anthology*, edited by Robert Stevenson. Washington, DC: General Secretariat, Organization of American States, 1975.

- Stockholm Ensemble Villancico. *Baroque Music of the Conquistadors*, 2000.

———. "No hay zagal como Gilillo"; "Christus natus est nobis." In *La música de México. III, Antología. 1, Periodo virreinal*, edited by Miguel Alcázar, J. Jesús Estrada, and E. Thomas Stanford. Mexico City: Instituto de Investigaciones Estéticas, Universidad Nacional Autónoma de México, 1987.

- Angelicum de Puebla / Schola Cantorum de Mexico. *México Barroco / Puebla I: Maitines de Navidad, 1653. Juan Gutiérrez de Padilla*, 1994.

Jerusalem y Stella, Ignacio de. "Cherubes y pastores." In *La música de México. III, Antología. 1, Periodo virreinal*, edited by Miguel Alcázar, J. Jesús Estrada, and E. Thomas Stanford. Mexico City: Instituto de Investigaciones Estéticas, Universidad Nacional Autónoma de México, 1987.

- Syntagma Musicum. *Convidando está la noche: Música europea y colonial latinoamericana de los siglos XVII y XVIII*, 2020.

Leonarda, Isabella. *Beatus vir*, op. 19, no. 4. In *Isabella Leonarda: Selected Compositions*, edited by Stewart Carter. Madison, WI: A-R Editions, 1997.

- *Tesori del Piemonte, Vol. 5: Leonarda: La Musa Novarese*, 1997.

Meda, Bianca Maria. *Cari musici*. Edited by Robert Kendrick. Bryn Mawr, PA: Hildegard Publishing Company, 1998.

- Bizzarrie Armoniche. *Donne Barocche*, 2010.

Rossi, Camilla de. *Il sacrifizio di Abramo: Vienna, 1708*. Edited and translated by Barbara Garvey Jackson. Fayetteville, AR: ClarNan Editions, 1984.

- Manfred Cordes. *Rossi: Il sacrifizio di Abramo*, 2000.

Sumaya (Zumaya) Manuel de. *Misa de tercer tono*. In *Misas de Manuel de Sumaya: Archivo musical de la catedral de Oaxaca*, edited by Aurelio Tello. Mexico City: Instituto Nacional de Bellas Artes, Centro Nacional de Investigación, Documentación e Información Musical Carlos Chávez, 1996.

- Ensemble Elyma. *Musique à la Cathédrale d'Oaxaca*, 2004.

———. *Resuenen los clarines*. Edited by Sarah Riskind. Choral Public Domain Library. https://www.cpdl.org/wiki/images/1/15/Zumaya_Resuenen_los_Clarines.pdf)

- Banda Barroca La Folia and Coro Cantvs Firmvs. *Resuenen los clarines*. Live recording. YouTube. https://www.youtube.com/watch?v=fiYDsSZdeEY.

———. "Ya se eriza el copete; De las flores y estrellas." In *Villancicos from Mexico City*, edited by Drew Edward Davies. Middleton, WI: A-R Editions, 2019.

- Chanticleer. *Mission Road*, 2009.

Vizzana, Lucrezia Orsina. "O invictissima Christi martyr." In *Five Arias: Voice and Continuo*, edited by Craig Monson. Bryn Mawr, PA: Hildegard Publishing Company, 1998.

* Cappella Artemisia. *Canti nel Chiostro: Musiche nei monasteri femminili del '600 a Bologna*, 2005.

Instrumental

Leonarda, Isabella. *Sonata duodecima from opus 16 (1693), for violin and continuo*. Edited by Barbara Garvey Jackson. Ottawa: Dovehouse Editions, 1983.

* Bizzarrie Armoniche. *Donne Barocche*, 2010.

———. *Sonata Terza, op. 16, for two violins, cello or gamba, and keyboard*. Edited by Caroline Cunningham. Bryn Mawr, PA: Hildegard Publishing Company, 1997.

* Cappella Strumentale del Duomo di Novara. *Isabella Leonarda: Sonate a 1, 2, 3 e 4 istromenti, Op. 16*, 2012.

Murcia, Santiago de. "Jácaras por la E; Marionas por la B; Cumbé por la A." In *Cifras selectas de guitarra*, edited by Alejandro Vera. Middleton, WI: A-R Editions, 2010.

* Paul O'Dette. *¡Jácaras!—18th Century Spanish Baroque Guitar Music of Santiago de Murcia*, 1998.

Selected Secondary Sources

Baker, Geoffrey, and Tess Knighton, eds. *Music and Urban Society in Colonial Latin America*. Cambridge: Cambridge University Press, 2011.

* Tess Knighton, "Music and Ritual in Urban Spaces: The Case of Lima, c. 1600," 21–42.

Brill, Mark. "The Oaxaca Cathedral *Examen de oposición*: The Quest for a Modern Style." *Latin American Music Review / Revista de Música Latinoamericana* 26, no. 1 (2005): 1–22.

Budasz, Rogério. "Black Guitar-Players and Early African-Iberian Music in Portugal and Brazil." *Early Music* 35, no. 1 (2007): 3–22.

Cashner, Andrew A. "Imitating Africans, Listening for Angels: A Slaveholder's Fantasy of Social Harmony in an 'Ethnic Villancico' from Colonial Puebla (1652)." *Journal of Musicology* 38, no. 2 (2021): 141–82.

Castagna, Paulo. "The Use of Music by the Jesuits in the Conversion of the Indigenous Peoples of Brazil." In *The Jesuits: Cultures, Sciences, and the Arts, 1540–1773*, edited by John W. O'Malley, Gauvin Alexander Bailey, Steven J. Harris, and T. Frank Kennedy, 641–58. Toronto: University of Toronto Press, 1999.

Chávez Bárcenas, Ireri E. "Native Song and Dance Affect in Seventeenth-Century Christian Festivals in New Spain." In *Acoustemologies in Contact: Sounding Subjects and Modes of Listening in Early Modernity*, edited by Emily Wilbourne and Suzanne G. Cusick, 37–64. Cambridge: OpenBook Publishers, 2021.

Coelho, Victor Anand. "Music in New Worlds." In *The Cambridge History of Seventeenth-Century Music*, edited by Tim Carter and John Butt, 88–110. Cambridge: Cambridge University Press, 2006.

Damon-Guillot, Anne. "Sounds of Hell and Sounds of Eden: Sonic Worlds in Ethiopia in the Catholic Missionary Context, Seventeenth and Eighteenth Centuries." In *Toward an Anthropology of Ambient Sound*, edited by Christine Guillebaud, 39–55. New York: Routledge, 2017.

Gasta, Chad M. "Public Reception, Politics, and Propaganda in Torrejón's *loa* to *La púrpura de la rosa,* the First New World Opera." *Latin American Theatre Review* 37, no. 1 (Fall 2003): 43–60.

Goodman, Glenda. "'But They Differ from Us in Sound': Indian Psalmody and the Soundscape of Colonialism, 1651–1675." *The William and Mary Quarterly* 69, no. 4 (October 2012): 793–822.

Gough, Melinda J. "Marie de Medici's 1605 *ballet de la reine* and the Virtuosic Female Voice." *Early Modern Women* 7 (2012): 127–56.

Head, Raymond. "Corelli in Calcutta: Colonial Music-Making in India during the 17th and 18th Centuries." *Early Music* 13, no. 4 (November 1985): 548–53.

Irving, David R.M. "The Dissemination and Use of Early Music Books in Early Modern Asia." *Early Music History* 28 (2009): 39–59.

———. "Historical and Literary Vestiges of the Villancico in the Early Modern Philippines." In *Devotional Music in the Iberian World, 1450–1800: The Villancico and Related Genres*, edited by Tess Knighton and Álvaro Torrente, 363–98. Burlington, VT: Ashgate, 2007.

Jooste, Fanie. "The Primary Influence on South African Wind Music of the Seventeenth and Eighteenth Centuries." *Journal of Band Research* 26, no. 2 (Spring 1991): 54–65.

Kendrick, Robert. "The Traditions of Milanese Convent Music and the Sacred Dialogues of Chiara Margarita Cozzolani." In *The Crannied Wall: Women, Religion, and the Arts in Early Modern Europe*, edited by Craig A. Monson, 211–33. Ann Arbor: University of Michigan Press, 1992.

Leaver, Robin A. "More than Simple Psalm-Singing in English: Sacred Music in Early Colonial America." *Yale Journal of Music & Religion* 1, no. 1 (2015): 63–80.

Mann, Kristin. *The Power of Song: Music and Dance in the Mission Communities of Northern New Spain, 1590–1810*. Stanford, CA: Stanford University Press, 2010.

- Chapter 2, "Liturgical and Religious Music in Europe, 1500–1800"
- Chapter 3, "Musical Cultures Meet"

Nunn, Erich. "'A Great Addition to Their Harmony': Plantation Slavery and Musical Exchange in Seventeenth-Century Barbados." *The Global South* 10, no. 2 (Fall 2016): 27–47.

Page, Janet K. "'A Lovely and Perfect Music': Maria Anna von Raschenau and the Music at the Viennese Convent of St Jakob auf der Hülben." *Early Music* 38, no. 3 (August 2010): 403–21.

Porter, Cecelia Hopkins. *Five Lives in Music: Women Performers, Composers, and Impresarios from the Baroque to the Present.* Urbana: University of Illinois Press, 2012.

- Chapter 1, "Duchess Sophie-Elisabeth: Composer, Harpsichordist, and Impresario in the North German Baroque"

Ramos-Kittrell, Jesús A. "Music, Liturgy, and Devotional Piety in New Spain: Baroque Religious Culture and the Re-evaluation of Religious Reform during the 18th Century." *Latin American Music Review / Revista de Música Latinoamericana* 31, no. 1 (2010): 79–100.

Stein, Louise K., and José Máximo Leza, "Opera, Genre, and Context in Spain and Its American Colonies." In *The Cambridge Companion to Eighteenth-Century Opera*, edited by Anthony R. DelDonna and Pierpaolo Polzonetti, 244–69. Cambridge: Cambridge University Press, 2009.

Urrows, David Francis. "The Pipe Organ of the Baroque Era in China," In *China and the West: Music, Representation, and Reception*, edited by Yang Hon-Lun and Michael Saffle, 21–48. Ann Arbor: University of Michigan Press, 2017.

Vera, Alejandro. *The Sweet Penance of Music: Musical Life in Colonial Santiago de Chile.* New York: Oxford University Press, 2020.

- Chapters organized by location of music making (cathedral, religious houses, private homes, etc.)

Yelloly, Margaret. "'The Ingenious Miss Turner': Elizabeth Turner (*d* 1756), Singer, Harpsichordist and Composer." *Early Music* 33, no. 1 (2005): 65–79.

3 Music between 1750 and 1815

Introduction

Many students do not associate the turbulent history that they know from this era, particularly the American and French Revolutions, with the seemingly placid and sometimes formulaic music of the Viennese Classicists. The late eighteenth century was a tumultuous period when European alliances shifted dramatically, monarchies fell or were weakened, and colonialism and slavery perpetuated the oppression of many people around the world.

From the perspective of Europeans, the "known" world continued to expand as explorers such as James Cook encountered people all over the planet. Colonization efforts begun in the sixteenth century persisted and, inevitably, conflicts arose between the major European powers, as well as between Indigenous people and settlers. The Seven Years' War (1756–63), in many ways the first global conflict, caused the realignment of European alliances with Great Britain emerging as a pre-eminent world power at the expense of France. The American and French Revolutions, meanwhile, saw Enlightenment ideas applied to new governmental systems.

Western classical music continued to be important to cultural and religious life in European colonies around the world. In many colonies, particularly those of the Spanish and Portuguese Empires, religious institutions had long required music for their services and celebrations but by 1750 urban centers had developed to the point that music was also a central part of their civic identities. The musical landscapes of these cities were shaped by the cultural values of the European, enslaved, and Indigenous people who lived there. In cities with large European populations, such as in Calcutta at the end of the century, some families re-created the home-based music making that existed in Europe.[1] They played music imported from Europe as well

DOI: 10.4324/9781003044635-4

as new works by local composers. Vocal music could be in European or Indigenous languages. Because of shared personnel, connections were forged between the cities of Europe and institutions in colonial centers. For instance, the Italian flute player Domenico Saccomano was part of the opera orchestra at Buen Retiro in Madrid before moving to Buenos Aires in the late 1750s where he founded the Teatro de Operas y Comedias. Composer Bartolomeo Massa, also Italian born, managed this theater and others in Lima from 1759 until after 1777. They brought the Italianate operatic style that was popular at the time in Madrid to the colonies.[2] While some colonial compositions may have been old-fashioned compared to European trends, many musical centers had access to music by contemporary composers and produced pieces that incorporated Classic-era innovations.

In some colonies, musicians were predominately white, whether they were born in the colony or in Europe, but in others, such as in the area that is now Brazil, most musicians were non-white, often of African descent or mixed race. There are records of orchestras staffed by enslaved people that played European music in places as disparate as Brazil, South Africa, and Java. These orchestras performed music to accompany activities such as dancing, during meals, and at public events.[3] Non-white musicians worked within institutions that imposed European-style music as part of a project of colonial subjugation, but at the same time they often found ways to insert meaning and musical elements from their own cultures. According to D.R.M. Irving, "the porous nature of intercultural frontiers and the resulting plurality of musical styles became chief characteristics of many early modern colonial cultures."[4]

The ideas promoted by Enlightenment philosophers exerted enormous influence over many aspects of European life. Enlightenment ideals of acceptance of difference, interest in women's capacity for achievement, and devotion to scientific discovery to combat deeply entrenched social myths could have resulted in reforms to governments and institutions that promoted equality. However, these ideas were put into practice within the existing framework of hierarchical governmental and social norms that were based upon the supremacy of white men. For a short time, some women and people of color profited from the idealism of the era and were able to carve out careers in music that might have been out of reach in the early nineteenth century. White women, in particular, benefitted from two structural changes in the period that afforded them more access to musical training and the ability to demonstrate professional-level skill. First, strictures against women participating in public activities, including concert performance and composition, eased somewhat, especially for single women. Second, the substantial economic gains made by the middle class meant families had money and time to devote to musical training (in some cases even composition lessons) for women. A refined education for a genteel girl now included the type of musical tuition once reserved for the wealthy and the nobility.

Locales & Locations

European courts were no longer the center of instrumental musical production, with more composers and performers earning money through public concerts. In London and Paris, for example, a network of public and semi-private spaces opened. While concert halls that sold tickets to anyone who could afford the price of a seat existed, many more performances took place in private ballrooms or salons where admission might be charged, but tickets were only available to invited participants. Musical patronage expanded from the nobility, the state, or the church to include a wider circle of people who sponsored concerts. Salons or semi-private concerts allowed patrons (many of whom were women) to enhance their social status and become leaders in the intellectual and musical lives of their cities, while fully public ticketed events also developed with the profits going to an impresario or concert space (such as London's Vauxhall Gardens). Semi-private spaces were ideal venues for white women and people of color to perform and to have their compositions heard. In a few cases, the theater also provided a home for women composers. For example, in Revolutionary-era France, women composers and librettists enjoyed a short-lived but intense period of access to operatic composition when at least fifty-four operas were written by twenty-three women between 1770 and 1820. These musicians took advantage of the Revolution's egalitarian rhetoric to claim a place within operatic institutions and networks of composers and librettists in Paris. Two operas by women, Julie Candeille's *Catherine, ou la belle fermière* (1793) and *Sapho* (1795) by Constance de Salm were among the most popular dramatic works in Paris when they premiered. These women also profited from a greater presence of women in literature, visual arts, and in the intellectual life of Paris at the time.[5]

Forms & Factions

In some colonies, most working musicians were of African descent, mixed race, or Indigenous. While colonial governments were dedicated to upholding and enforcing imperial governments and European culture, local inhabitants both resisted and accommodated the imperatives of the state through music. The amount of influence from Indigenous or African music on European classical-style compositions varied widely across the colonies depending upon local conditions. For example, in colonial Manila, the interaction of European and Indigenous musical practices was more complex than simply the domination of Spanish music as an extension of the colonial project. Although music existed within colonial regulations that shaped and constrained the social, religious, and political life of Manila and the Philippines, there was still room for a multiplicity of artistic styles. D.R.M. Irving contends that music in the Philippines underwent a process of "hispanization" that he argues "was not a clear-cut case of 'imposition,'" but rather also reflected that Filipinos wanted to take part in aspects of European culture and thus "adopted and adapted" music of Europe to their own uses.[6]

Responses & Reception

The end of the eighteenth century saw some European Black musicians participate in classical music who were not part of military musical establishments or colonial music making. For instance, George Polgreen Bridgetower (1779–1860), a violinist of mixed race, began studying the instrument when his father (a native of Barbados) was Prince Nicolas Esterházy's personal page at the same time Joseph Haydn was working for the nobleman. By 1789, Bridgetower and his father were in London where they took advantage of the complex web of public and private concerts and networks of patronage among the nobility and professional musicians to promote the eleven-year-old's musical career. Reviews of Bridgetower's early concerts reveal that critics were impressed with the prodigy's skill, but the exotic appeal of the boy they called the "African Prince" also drove some of the interest in him. It was the patronage of the Prince of Wales, who oversaw Bridgetower's career and provided him with musical and academic tutors, that provided Bridgetower with the prestige as well as the access to the kind of education he needed to thrive in the European musical marketplace. Today his fame rests on Beethoven's dedication of the *Kreutzer* sonata to him in 1803, but Bridgetower's life story is an excellent example of the importance of canny marketing and well-connected patronage in establishing a solo music career, especially for musicians who did not have the advantage of family connections.[7]

Notes

1 Ian Woodfield, *Music of the Raj: A Social and Economic History of Music in Late Eighteenth Century Anglo-Indian Society* (New York: Oxford University Press, 2000), 3.
2 Louise K. Stein and José Máximo Leza, "Opera, Genre, and Context in Spain and Its American Colonies," in *The Cambridge Companion to Eighteenth-Century Opera*, ed. Anthony R. DelDonna and Pierpaolo Polzonetti (Cambridge: Cambridge University Press, 2009), 244–69, at 265–66.
3 Danielle Fosler-Lussier, *Music on the Move* (Ann Arbor: University of Michigan Press, 2020), 26.
4 D.R.M. Irving, *Colonial Counterpoint: Music in Early Modern Manila* (New York: Oxford University Press, 2010), 3.
5 Jacqueline Letzter and Robert Adelson, *Women Writing Opera: Creativity and Controversy in the Age of the French Revolution* (Berkeley: University of California Press, 2001).
6 Irving, *Colonial Counterpoint*, 11.
7 This paragraph is based on Josephine R.B. Wright, "George Polgreen Bridgetower: An African Prodigy in England 1789–99," *The Musical Quarterly* 66, no. 1 (January 1980): 65–82.

Lesson 3.1: Marianna Martines, Sonata in E Major

Background

Austrian composer, singer, and keyboardist Marianna Martines (1744–1812) was highly esteemed during the Classic period. Supported primarily by the patronage of Pietro Metastasio (a poet and well-known librettist), she studied voice as a teenager and collaborated with a young Joseph Haydn.[1] Metastasio continued to sponsor the development of her musical gifts into young adulthood, as she composed (among other works) four masses, a chamber cantata, and a keyboard sonata by her twentieth birthday. In 1773, she achieved the high honor of being the first woman elected to the Accademia Filarmonica (Philharmonic Academy) of Bologna, a society of composers and musical aficionados.[2] A skilled pianist, she performed duets with Mozart in the 1770s. Her reputation as a composer and performer allowed her to ascend into the upper ranks of Viennese aristocracy. Although her last dated composition is a chamber cantata from 1786, she remained active in social and musical circles until the turn of the nineteenth century.[3]

Sonata in E Major, First Movement (1763)

Our discussion of this movement begins with the larger formal scheme and will continue through selected details that add nuance and vitality. Irving Godt notes:

The Sonata in E makes use in all three movements of a kind of sonata form with an exposition in which the opening theme returns in the second theme area (that is, as part of a group of melodies in the dominant) ... The [first] movement's strengths are its unpretentiousness and vigorous rhythms.[4]

While agreeing with Godt, the form diagram below offers a fuller account of the movement's form (see Table 3.1). Two melodic/thematic ideas constitute the main characters of the movement: (1) the primary theme (mm. 1–8) and the cascading, arpeggiated sixteenth-note figures (mm. 9–14). These two ideas along with the relative strength of cadential arrivals form the basis for the secondary theme areas of the exposition (mm. 32–50) and recapitulation (mm. 95–106), excepting the cadential tag figures that round out those sections. As usual, the first half of this movement is characterized by global harmonic motion from the tonic to the dominant.

Martines's move away from the tonic key is subtle and effective. After the imperfect authentic cadence in E major at measure 8, there are three arrivals on B major chords that gradually increase in strength. The first cadence occurs at the end of the cascading, sixteenth note figures (Episode 1), sounding and functioning more like a half cadence in E major (m. 15). Martines provides the listener with expectations associated with secondary themes, but the material quickly moves away from conventional practice. The next transitional episode features new melodic ideas and a chromatic descent in the right hand. The left hand ascends in contrary motion, completing the phrase on an E major chord. The three-measure extension offers a slightly stronger arrival on B major because of the emphasis of the A# in the bass for two of the three measures (mm. 22–23). Tension is generated by the arrival of the E major chord in the first phrase and the immediate shift to a chromatic chord (vii°7 in B) as well as the increase in rhythmic density in the right hand. Episode 3 consists of leaping figures and a thinner texture. The arrival to B major is strongest and most convincing here because of the prevalence of the leading tone and the strength of the perfect authentic cadence (m. 32).

Martines's treatment of rhythm in the second and third transitional episodes is also noteworthy. Each episode is seven measures in length. The contrasting melodic ideas and dramatic bass leap in Episode 2 somewhat diminish the conceivable hitch of an asymmetrical phrase structure. However, the absolute thwarting of listener expectations in Episode 3 offers elements of convention and surprise, as Martines' cadence elides with the beginning of the second theme area.

Regarding the second half of the piece (e.g. Development and Recapitulation), events unfold in a conventional manner. L. Poundie

Burstein's analysis of Martines's Sonata in A major notes a distinctive alignment with Heinrich Christopher Koch's theories on sonata form during that time:

> Koch mentions the following strategy: "After it has begun in the key of the fifth, the theme may be modified so that it ends again in the main key, [then] there is a modulation from the main key into one of the minor keys [vi, ii, or iii]." ... And this is precisely what happens in the second half of Martines's sonata movement.[5]

Martines follows a similar model in the E major sonata. A-natural predominates in the ending of the phrase group at the beginning of the development, suggesting a return to E major. This return is not without question, as the phrase group ends with a half cadence. Following a series of sequences based on material from transitional episodes, Martines briefly establishes C# minor before continuing sequential activity and ultimately preparing the recapitulation—which is also initiated with an elided cadence. The sonata concludes with a conventional recapitulation of the primary theme and material from the secondary key area in the tonic.

The Sonata in E is a good piece for either an introduction to the sonata principle or to supplement discussions on the topic. The first movement aligns well with conventions associated with keyboard sonatas of the time. The main key areas are I (tonic) and V (dominant). Using the Martines to introduce the sonata principle affords the opportunity to focus on the strength of cadences and the consequential departure from and return to the tonic key. As this piece highlights statements of the primary thematic idea in the tonic and dominant, discussions of the sonata principle could be centered on harmonic structure rather than melodic differences between themes which many students rely on to identify thematic areas. Whereas a number of classic sonata realizations espouse contrast between themes, the Martines sonata highlights the tonal contrasts/conflicts that also give energy and drama to the formal scheme. As a supplemental piece for sonata form discussions, the features of the Martines could be likened to monothematic expositions as sometimes employed by Haydn and Mozart.

Locales & Locations

Martines's musical reputation and inheritance from Metastasio situated her among the leading aristocrats in Vienna during the late eighteenth century. According to Godt:

Table 3.1 Form Chart, Martines Sonata in E Major, first movement.

Section	Event	Measures	Main Keys	Comments
	Primary Theme	1–8	E major	
	Transition	9–32	E major (I); B major (V)	Episode 1 (mm. 9–17); sequential sixteenth note figures concluding with tonicization of B major. Episode 2 (mm. 18–24); chromatic progression which ultimately tonicizes B major. Episode 3 (mm. 25–32); leaping melody/diatonic progression establishes B major with elided PAC.
	Secondary Theme (Area)	32–39	B major (V)	Near literal reiteration of primary theme
	Secondary Theme (ind.)	39–50		Rapid sixteenth note figures with diatonic descent in lowest voice (figuration borrowed from Episode 1)
	Closing	50–54	B major (V)	Repetitions of cadential tag motif
Development	Primary Th. (dev.)	55–62	B major (V) to E major (I)	Restatement of primary theme; abruptly modulates to E major
	Developmental Episodes	63–78	E major (I) to C-sharp minor (vi)	Material from Episode 1 and Episode 3; treated falling fifth sequences with chromatic harmonies
		78–88	C-sharp minor (vi) to V of E major	Melodic ideas borrowed from Episode 2; treated with sequences, ending with altered restatement of melodic material and diatonic progression of Episode 3. Elided PAC initiates recapitulation.
Recapitulation	Primary Theme	88–95	E major (I)	
	Secondary Theme (ind.)	95–106		
	Closing	106–110		

the ennoblement of her family may have opened to her aristocratic academies that had previously been inaccessible and made her own academies more attractive to members of the nobility. That, together with the substantial inheritance…may have encouraged her to increase the lavishness of her academies to the point where, by the 1790s, they occupied a prominent place in Vienna's musical landscape.[6]

She also occupied a large living space that facilitated these extravagant events. Among the notable guests at Martines's parties were tenor Michael Kelly and Wolfgang Amadeus Mozart. Some of Mozart's later piano sonatas for four hands may have been composed with Martines in mind, as they performed some of his piano duets at her parties.[7] The later four hands pieces by Mozart (K. 497 and K. 521) are more mature works that feature brilliant technical passages and moments of melodic eloquence. If they were indeed composed for Martines and her gatherings, this speaks to her accomplishment as a keyboardist as well. There is no record of her holding a musical appointment in the noble courts of Vienna, but her level of achievement and her position as an important academy hostess afforded her the opportunity for engagement with nobility in private spaces.

Further Consideration: While musical academies/parties were commonplace in Vienna during that time, it is unlikely that many were held in spaces owned by women. Did Martines teach? Yes, but ironically, most of her protégés were voice students. Matthew Head gives a detailed account of Martines's strong reputation as a singer and interpreter of Italian opera.[8] Women often came to prominence because they hosted academies and parties (or salons) rather than as public performers. Why would these private spaces be more open to the active participation by women than public venues?

Forms & Factions

Considered among the greatest librettists of Italian opera, Metastasio enjoyed considerable wealth and authority in the artistic circles of Vienna. Martines's long-standing ties to the Italian writer lasted from her childhood to his death in 1782. Her family shared a floor with him at a large apartment building (Altes Michaelerhaus) in Vienna, and he was an early, strong, and enduring supporter of the young Martines. While the social circles Metastasio moved in may have involved nobility, he was not of a royal lineage. Patrons supported Metastasio in his younger years because of his talent as a poet which he parlayed into a court appointment. Although the court supported much of the musical activity in Vienna during the Classic Period, Metastasio's sphere of influence encompassed academies and other institutions that promoted young Martines's compositional and performance aspirations. The facility and musicality of the Sonata in E and her early vocal works must have shown considerable promise to Metastasio.

Further Consideration: Surveying Metastasio's output and the composers who incorporated his work into their operas could shed light on the strength of his reputation and influence; it could also serve as a pivot into discussions about opera in the eighteenth century. There is no evidence that Martines composed an opera, but her catalog includes a number of works for voice (including Italian arias based on texts by Metastasio). Challenge your students to imagine why Martines might never have written opera and why women often confined themselves to smaller forms. (Because there was so little chance that an opera theater would perform a work by a woman?)

Responses & Reception

As the Sonata in E is considered an early work, the piece could be used as an introduction to the early years of Martines's life when she was just becoming established as a composer and performer. She probably wrote this sonata when she was nineteen years old or younger. Many of her early works were sacred, so this solo keyboard work sits in slight contrast to much of her output during those years. Her loyal supporter, Pietro Metastasio probably recommended her to the Accademia Filarmonica of Bologna. It was her liturgical compositions, however, that ultimately led to her nomination and election as the first woman member of the highly revered Accademia Filarmonica of Bologna in 1773.[9] She composed numerous keyboard sonatas, arias, psalms, masses, and keyboard concerti before her election.

Further Consideration: According to Godt, the earliest correspondence between Martines and the facilitators of the Accademia Filarmonica occurred in 1773.[10] It is presumed that Metastasio submitted scores to the jury/governing body on her behalf, as written correspondence between the Accademia and Martines appears to have begun after she was elected. Discuss the benefits (and drawbacks) of networking systems that had to have been in place for women and persons of color to be considered for and accepted into the loftier statuses of musicians and artists of that era.

Sonata in E Major, first movement by Marianna Martines

Notes

1 Irving Godt, *Marianna Martines: A Woman Composer in the Vienna of Mozart and Haydn* (Rochester, NY: University of Rochester Press, 2010), 20–22.

2 Godt, *Marianna Martines*, 138.

3 L. Poundie Burstein, "'Zierlichkeit und Genie': Grace and Genius in Marianna Martines's Sonata in A Major," in *Analytical Essays on Music by Women Composers: Secular and Sacred Music to 1900*, ed. Laurel Parsons and Brenda Ravenscroft (New York: Oxford University Press, 2018), 131–45.

4 Godt, *Marianna Martines*, 53.
5 Burstein, "Marianna Martines's Sonata in A Major," 139.
6 Godt, *Marianna Martines*, 194.
7 Godt, 197.
8 Matthew Head, *Sovereign Feminine: Music and Gender in Eighteenth-Century Germany* (Berkeley: University of California Press, 2013), 38–42.
9 Godt, *Marianna Martines*, 137–38.
10 Godt, *Marianna Martines*, 135.

Lesson 3.2: Sonata in E-flat Major, H. XVI: 52 by Joseph Haydn: A Study in Private and Public/Masculine and Feminine

Background

The idea of the public instrumental concert that anyone could attend provided they could afford a ticket was a new concept in the Classic period. London was one of the first cities to have an active public concert life, but many of the events that required tickets to access were not as public as they might seem at first glance. For many concerts only people with invitations could apply to buy a ticket, and many of these events were held in private homes rather than public spaces. Often women served as impresarios, promoters, and hosts for these types of concerts.

While these semi-public concerts were developing in London and other large European cities, musical study had become a crucial part of the education of middle- and upper-class girls. To serve this large consumer base, composers churned out hundreds, if not thousands, of piano sonatas and piano trios that amateur-level pianists, violinists, and cellists could perform at home in their parlors as an afternoon or after-dinner diversion for acquaintances and suitors. Noting the dichotomy between technically difficult, bombastic, harmonically adventuresome piano pieces, and the easier, modest sonatas marketed to the home pianist, some musicologists have claimed that the bigger pieces were designed for public presentation by professional male performers, while the smaller works were compositions suitable for amateur women in small private spaces. This conception equates difficult, aggressive music, professionalism, and public performance with men and private performance, amateur musicianship and undemanding music with women. More recent scholarship has cast doubt on these easy dichotomies (public vs. private, amateur vs. professional, and men vs. women) as it has become clear that women performed complicated, technically demanding pieces in venues open to a select audience in a professional environment, and that men performed simpler, less challenging music in more public concerts.[1]

The Sonata in E-flat Major, H XVI: 52 by Joseph Haydn is a good example of a substantial piece by a canonical composer that confounds stereotypes about the nature of eighteenth-century concert life, professionalism, and these issues' relationships to gender. The sonata is expansive, quite difficult technically, and aesthetically sophisticated. It seems to be a textbook example of a piece designed for public performance in a large venue. Haydn dedicated this sonata to Therese Jansen Bartolozzi (c. 1770–1843), perhaps one of the best pianists in London at the end of the eighteenth century. There are only three recorded examples of her playing in semi-public concerts for a restricted audience, otherwise she apparently only performed in private settings or perhaps ticketed concerts that were never advertised to the public.[2] Yet Haydn not only recorded her as one of the pianists he met during his first visit to London in 1791, he was also a witness to her marriage to the engraver Gaetano Bartolozzi during his second visit in 1795. Jan Dussek and Muzio Clementi (her teacher) also dedicated some of their most difficult piano music to Bartolozzi. Dussek wrote much more demanding music for Bartolozzi than he did for his own use as a professional pianist. Because most performances in private homes were never commented upon in the press, we have very little documentary evidence about Bartolozzi's professional life. Scattered mentions of her in diaries and memoirs from the period paint her as a skilled pianist who performed regularly in exclusive, private settings where she had access to the most celebrated male composers and performers of the period.[3]

In this era, dedications were part of the musical advertising for a piece and could indicate a connection between the composer and a prominent figure with whom the potential consumer also wanted to be associated.[4] This suggests that Bartolozzi was well known within musical circles in London and that her reputation would enhance Haydn's standing and the piece's cultural capital. The Viennese edition of the E-flat Sonata has a different dedicatee—Magdalena von Kurzböck.[5] Similar to Bartolozzi, she was a student of Clementi's, was a celebrated pianist who performed in private spaces in Vienna, and was part of Haydn's circle in Austria. This change suggests that Bartolozzi was famous enough in London for the dedication to mean something to consumers there, but that Kurzböck was a better choice to entice buyers in Vienna.

The Sonata in E-flat Major is technically demanding, and the first movement is unusual in form with a particularly long and fragmented secondary theme and truncated recapitulation. The entire piece is also innovative, particularly harmonically, with several significant fermatas on G Major in the first movement; a second movement in E major that begins as if it will be a theme and variation, although it is not; and an inventive rondo that subverts the listener's expectations melodically, harmonically, and formally.[6]

Locales & Locations

Scholars tend to associate small-scale pieces with smaller performance venues, smaller venues with private homes, and private concerts with lower prestige. The cultural context surrounding the Sonata in E-flat demonstrates that these associations are not always correct. Although there was no private home in London that could rival the large outdoor spaces of the Vauxhall Pleasure Gardens, there were more restricted venues in the city that could accommodate at least 400 people. Despite being the biggest and most famous concert site in the city, the Vauxhall Pleasure Gardens was probably one of the least prestigious venues in London, as it was a known haunt for thieves and prostitutes. Respectable women were warned away from the space entirely or cautioned to keep to lighted areas with their chaperones so that they would not be attacked. A small salon performance hosted by the Prince of Wales, on the other hand, could easily boast the most prestigious and most famous musicians in the city performing the type of large, expansive pieces that may seem too big and exciting for an intimate venue. The presence of nobility among the guests and performers assured that this entirely private performance would have been of very high quality as well as one of the most notable concert venues in London, highly sought after by every performer in the area. It also indicates that it would be a mistake to think about the advent of public concerts as the beginning of some kind of "democratization of classical music" as it moved from the preserve of the court to the concert hall. In the late eighteenth century, the potential audience for many concerts in music halls, private homes, and social clubs was purposefully limited to people of the upper class and would have been just as out of reach for regular concertgoers as an invitation to court.

Further Consideration: Challenge your students to think about concert life today—do we have "private" or semi-public concerts that are only open to certain people? What kinds of venues host concerts? How is classical music marketed today? Has the typical classical music audience changed much since the late-eighteenth century? How do musicians today signal their connections and musical tastes to a potential audience?

Forms & Factions

In the late eighteenth century, middle- and upper-class women were expected to stay away from the sorts of public engagements typically associated with men such as working outside of the home, entering the political realm, or performing on the public stage. A woman who transgressed these boundaries faced the possibility of sacrificing her reputation as a respectable woman and a profound loss of status. Some women, however, were able to work within the era's gender norms while still fashioning a professional career. For instance, Theresa Cornelys presented concerts at the Carlisle House, her home in London, beginning in 1760. She hired J.C. Bach and C.F. Abel to program a concert series for Carlisle House in 1765 (now famous as the Bach-Abel Series) and promoted those concerts for three years until the two men took control of the series and moved it to the Hanover Square Rooms. Only those women with enough social standing to be included on Cornelys' "ladies list" and their (male or female) guests were allowed to buy an expensive ticket to one of her presentations.[7] These exclusive events were sought-after social occasions for the audience, as well as important performance opportunities for professional women instrumentalists like Bartolozzi and Kurzböck who often could not or chose not to play in more "public" events because of the risk to their respectability, especially after they married.[8] Cornelys supported her family and functioned as one of the most important of London's impresarios, yet by hosting concerts in her home and limiting the potential audience who could cross her threshold, she maintained her respectability.

Further Consideration: How might the prestige of certain genres of music (symphonic music, chamber music, opera, piano music, etc.) be related to gender and the accepted gender roles of a particular time period?

Responses & Reception

Our understanding of women's professional lives is constrained by a lack of documentation. Both Bartolozzi and Kurzböck seemed to have had active performance careers, but their accomplishments are difficult to assess because they, of necessity, stayed away from the type of events and publicity that were open to men. This limitation did not mean that their careers were secondary to men's, that they were not as skilled as men, or that they played more "intimate" repertory. In fact, men also wanted to appear in the sort of private spaces where many women performed. Some men even scaled back their public concerts to allow time to perform in salons and more exclusive venues. Meanwhile, women's private performances were neither advertised nor reviewed in the press. We must rely on anecdotal evidence (such as dedications) or first-hand accounts in letters or memoirs for a record of their activities. This evidence is incomplete in part because many people thought any mention of a woman's life in the print media would damage her reputation, especially if she was from the upper class or the aristocracy. This social norm means that women were routinely erased from the public record. While women salon hostesses, performers, and composers sometimes played a pivotal role in the cultural lives of their cities, it is difficult to recreate an accurate picture of that artistic landscape because so many of their activities took place behind closed doors.

Further Consideration: What kind of documents do we need to understand the cultural life of a particular area today? Talk to your students about the difficulty in truly understanding the concert life in this period—who the best performers were, what repertoire was played, and even when concerts were held—because private concerts were not covered by the press.

Notes

1 For three ways that musicologists have conceived of the relationship between concert life, gender, and musical compositions see László Somfai, *Keyboard Sonatas of Joseph Haydn: Instruments and Performance Practice, Genres and Styles* (Chicago, IL: University of Chicago Press, 1995); Michelle Fillion, "Intimate Expression for a Widening Public: The Keyboard Sonatas and Trios," in *The Cambridge Companion to Haydn*, ed. Caryl Clark (Cambridge: University of Cambridge Press, 2005), 126–37; Mary Hunter, "Haydn's London Piano Trios and His Salomon String Quartets: Private vs. Public?" in *Haydn and His World*, ed. Elaine Sisman (Princeton: Princeton University Press, 1997), 103–30.

2 Haydn also dedicated the Piano Sonata in C Major, H. XIV: 52 and three late piano trios to Bartolozzi which are all demanding technically and expressively. The piano trios stand out in a genre that at the end of the eighteenth century was usually characterized by much simpler compositions.

3 For more biographical information on Bartolozzi see W. Oliver Strunk, "Notes on a Haydn Autograph," *The Musical Quarterly* 20, no. 2 (April 1934): 192–205; Christopher Hogwood, *Haydn's Visits to England* (London: Thames and Hudson, 2009).

4 Emily Green, "A Patron among Peers: Dedications to Haydn and the Economy of Celebrity," *Eighteenth-Century Music* 8, no. 2 (2011): 215–37.

5 Very little information is available on Kurzböck (also spelled von Kurzbeck). Her father was a Viennese publisher and writer (Joseph Kurzböck) to whom Empress Maria Theresa gave a noble title. She and Haydn were so close that not long before he died, Kurzböck asked him to live with her, although he refused (H.C. Robbins Landon's, *Haydn: Chronicle and Works* (London: Thames and Hudson, 1994), Vol. 3, 452;

Vol. 5, 387n1). See also Rita Steblin, "Who was Beethoven's 'Elise'? A New Solution to the Mystery," *Musical Times* 155, no. 1927 (Summer 2014): 3–39.

6 See Lawrence Moss, "Haydn's Sonata Hob. XVI:52 (ChL. 62) in E-Flat Major: An Analysis of the First Movement," in *Haydn Studies: Proceedings of the International Haydn Conference, Washington, D.C., 1975*, ed. Jens Peter Larsen, Howard Serwer, and James Webster (New York: Norton, 1981), 496–501.

7 Simon McVeigh, *Concert Life in London from Mozart to Haydn* (Cambridge: Cambridge University Press, 1993), 38–44.

8 Nicholas Salwey, "Women Pianists in Late Eighteenth-Century London," in *Concert Life in Eighteenth-Century Britain*, ed. Susan Wollenberg and Simon McVeigh (Burlington, VT: Ashgate, 2004), 273–90.

Bibliography

Score/Recording

Orchestral

Saint-Georges, Joseph Bologne, Chevalier de. Symphony in G Major, op. 11, no. 1. In *Five Symphonic Works*, edited by Barry S. Brook and David Bain. New York: Garland, 1983.

- *Black Composers Series*, Vol. 1. Columbia Masterworks, 1974. Remastered by Sony Classical, 2019.

Solo Instruments and Orchestra

Agnesi, Maria Teresa. *Concerto in F Major for Harpsichord and Strings*. Louisville, KY: Ars Femina, 1993.

- *Note Femminili: Compositrici Lombarde dal XVII al XIX Secolo*, 2002.

Park, Maria Hester Reynolds. *Concerto for the Piano Forte or Harpsichord in E-flat Major*. Edited by Barbara Harbach. Pullman, WA: Vivace Press, 1993. Arranged for solo keyboard.

- Barbara Harbach. *18th Century Solo Harpsichord Music by Women Composers*, Vol. 2, 1993.

Saint-Georges, Joseph Bologne, Chevalier de. *Violin Concerto in A*, op. 5, no. 2. Edited by Allan Badley. Wellington, NZ: Artaria, 2004.

- Rachel Barton Pine. *Violin Concertos by Black Composers of the Eighteenth and Nineteenth Centuries*, 1997.

———. *Violin Concerto No. 9 in G*, op. 8. Edited by Allan Badley. Wellington, NZ: Artaria Editions, 1999.

- Takako Nishizaki. *Joseph Bologne, Chevalier de Saint-Georges: Violin Concertos*, 2001.

Sirmen, Maddalena Lombardini. Concerto no. 5 in B-Flat for Violin. In *Three Violin Concertos* [from op. 3]. Edited by Jane L. Berdes. Recent Researches in Music of the Classical Era 38. Madison, WI: A-R Editions, 1991.

- JoAnn Falletta. *Baroquen Treasures*, 1990.

Chamber Music for Strings

Saint-Georges, Joseph Bologne, Chevalier de. *String Quartet in C Major*, op. 1, no. 1. Edited by Neal Richardson and William Bauer. Louisville, KY: Africanus Editions, 1998.

- Paul Freeman. *Black Composers Series*, Vol. 1. Columbia Masterworks, 1974. Remastered by Sony Classical, 2019.

Sirmen, Maddalena Lombardini. *Six String Quartets*, op. 3. 2 vols. Edited by Sally Didrickson. Bryn Mawr, PA: Hildegard Publishing Company, 2002–2003.

- Allegri String Quartet. *Maddalena Lombardini Sirmen: The Six String Quartets*, 1994.

Chamber Music with Keyboard

Bon, Anna. *VI Sonate da Camera: per il Flauto Traversiere e Violoncello o Cembalo*. Edited by Barbara Jackson Garvey. Fayetteville, AR: ClarNan Editions, 1989.

- Ensemble Oberon. *Anna Bon: Sei Sonate da Camera per il Flauto Traversiere*, 2009.

Liebmann, Hélène Riese. *Grand Trio in A*, op. 11. Edited by Diana Ambache. Bryn Mawr, PA: Hildegard Publishing Company, 2003.

- *Hofkomponistinnen in Europa: aus Boudoir und Gärten*, Vol. 1, 1998.

Sancho, Ignatius. *Minuets for the Violin, Mandolin, German Flute, and Harpsichord*. IMSLP. https://imslp.org/wiki/Minuets,_etc._(Sancho,_Ignatius)

- Janise White. *Minuets & Optional Dances: Ignatius Sancho*, 2015.

Sonatas

Auenbrugger, Marianna von. *Sonata per il clavicembalo o forte piano*. Edited by Sylvia Glickman. Bryn Mawr, PA: Hildegard Publishing Company, 1990.

- Barbara Baird. *Vienna: Two Centuries of Harpsichord Music (1600–1800)*, 1995.

Barthélemon, Cecilia Maria. Sonatas, op. 1, no. 3 in E Major; op. 3 in G Major. In *Three Sonatas for Piano*, edited by Barbara Harbach. Pullman, WA: Vivace Press, 1995.

- *Hofkomponistinnen in Europa: aus Boudoir und Gärten*, Vol. 2, 1998. (Sonata in E Major)

- Barbara Harbach. *18th Century Women Composers: Music for Harpsichord*, vol. 2, 1993. (Sonata in G Major)

Bon, Anna. *Six Sonatas for Harpsichord or Piano*. Edited by Barbara Harbach. Pullman, WA: Vivace Press, 1995.

- Barbara Harbach. *Anna Bon di Venezia: Six Sonatas for Harpsichord, Op. 2*, 2008.

Dussek, Sophia Giustina Corri. *Sonata for Harp in C Minor*, op. 2 no. 3. Formerly attributed to J. L. Dussek. Edited by Nicanor Zabaleta. New York: Schott, 1954.

- Laura Zaerr. *L'autre jour—Harp Music of the 18th and 19th Centuries*, 1995.

———. *Sonata No. 1 in B-flat for Harp*, op. 2, no. 1. Formerly attributed to J. L. Dussek. New York: Lyra Music Co., 1978.

- Floraleda Sacchi. *Sophia Giustina Corri: Works for Solo Harp*, 2013.

Gambarini, Elisabetta de. *Lessons for Harpsichord*, op. I and op. II. Edited by Martha Secrest Asti. Bryn Mawr, PA: Hildegard Publishing Company, 1995.

- Paule von Parys. *Gambarini: Lessons for the Harpsichord*, 1998.

———. *Six Sonatas for Harpsichord or Piano*. Edited by Barbara Harbach. Pullman, WA: Vivace Press, 1994.

- Barbara Harbach. *Sonatas by Elizabeth*, 1995.

Hardin, Elizabeth. *Six Lessons for Harpsichord or Piano*. Edited by Barbara Harbach. Pullman, WA: Vivace Press, 1994.

- Barbara Harbach. *Sonatas by Elizabeth*, 1995.

Martines, Marianna. *Three Sonatas for Keyboard*. Edited by Shirley Bean. Bryn Mawr: Hildegard Publishing Company, 1994.

- Barbara Harbach. *Music for Solo Harpsichord by 18th Century Women Composers*, Vol. 1, 1995. (Sonata in E Major)
- Nuria Rial. *Marianna Martines: Il Primo Amore*, 2012. (Sonata in A Major)
- La Floridiana. *La Tempesta*, 2015. (Sonata in G Major)

Park, Maria Hester Reynolds. Sonata I in F Major, op. 4; Sonata in C Major, op. 7. In *Eighteenth Century Women Composers for the Harpsichord or Piano*, vol. 1, edited by Barbara Harbach. Pullman, WA: Vivace Press, 1992.

- Barbara Harbach. *Music for Solo Harpsichord by 18th Century Women Composers*, Vol. 1, 1995. (Sonata in F Major)
- Barbara Harbach. *18th Century Solo Harpsichord Music by Women Composers*, Vol. 2, 1993. (Sonata in C Major)

Other Keyboard Pieces

Álvares Pinto, Luís. *Lições de Solfejo*. Musica Brasilis. https://musicabrasilis.org.br/partituras/luis-alvares-pinto-25-licoes-de-solfejo

- Jeffrey Skidmore. *Brazilian Adventures*, 2015.

Auernhammer, Josepha Barbara von. *Sechs Variationen über ein ungarisches Thema*. Edited by Rosario Marciano. Kassel: Furore, 1998.

- Judith Pfeiffer. *Judith Pfeiffer*, 2002.

Saint-Georges, Joseph Bologne, Chevalier de. *Adagio in F Minor*. Edited by Dominique-René de Lerma. Bryn Mawr, PA: Merion Music, 1981.

- Teo Barry Vincent. *Classical Masters' Works: The Classical Era: 1750–1820*, Teo Barry Vincent, 2017.

Opera

Anna Amalia, Duchess of Saxe-Weimar. *Erwin und Elmire*. Edited by Peter Tregear. Kassel: Furore, 2011. (only excerpts recorded)

- Overture: Academy of Ancient Music. Live recording. YouTube. https://www.youtube.com/watch?v=WSCPBH88ZxM
- "Auf dem Land und in der Stadt": *Goethe-Lieder. Auf dem Land und in der Stadt*, 1995.
- "Ihr solltet geniessen": *Women's Voices: Five Centuries of Song*, 1996.
- "Sieh mich, Heil'ger, wie ich bin": *Lieder von Komponistinnen des 18. Und 19*, 1999.

Grétry, Lucile. *Le Mariage d'Antonio*. Edited by Robert Adelson. Middleton, WI: A-R Editions, 2008.

- Live recording. YouTube. https://www.youtube.com/watch?v=yIBPei-mA2WI&list=PLM826VW_qtnmpruE3wG9AZOu5GiFQpPAX&index=5&t=327s

Choral Works with Orchestra

Martines, Marianna. *In exitu Israel*. Edited by Shirley Bean. Fayetteville, AR: ClarNan Editions, 2012.

- Kölner Kurrende. *Psalmkantaten*, 1996.

Nunes Garcia, José Maurício. *Requiem in D Minor*. Edited by Cleofe Person de Mattos. Stuttgart, Germany: Carus Verlag, 1994.

- *Black Composers Series, Vol. 5*. Columbia Masterworks M 32781, 1974. Remastered by Sony Classical, 2019.

———. *Missa pastoril para noite de Natal*. Musica Brasilis. https://musicabrasilis.org.br/partituras/jose-mauricio-nunes-garcia-missa-pastoril-para-noite-de-natal

- Ensemble Turicum. *Jose Mauricio Nunes Garcia: Missa pastoril para noite de Natal*, 2002.

Other Choral Works

Álvares Pinto, Luís. "Beata Virgo" and "Oh! Pulchra es." In *Divertimentos Harmônicos*. Musica Brasilis. https://musicabrasilis.org.br/partituras/ luis-alvares-pinto-divertimentos-harmonicos

- Jeffrey Skidmore. *Brazilian Adventures*, 2015.

Solo Voices and Orchestra

Martines, Marianna. *La Tempesta*. Edited by Shirley Bean. Piano Reduction. Fayetteville, AR: ClarNan Editions, 2011.

- La Floridiana. *La Tempesta*, 2015.

Songs

Arnim, Bettine Brentano von. "Ach neige, du Schmerzenreiche"; "O schaudre nicht"; "Wanderers Nachtlied"; "An Luna." In *Goethe-Vertonungen für Singstimme und Klavier*. Edited by Renate Moering and Reinhard Schmiedel. Kassel: Furore, 1999.

- *Wie ein Cherub aus den Wolken: Hommage an Bettine von Arnim*, 2010.

Paradis, Maria Theresia von. *Zwölf Lieder auf ihrer Reise in Musik gesetzt: 1784– 86*. Edited by Hidemi Matsushita. Fayetteville, AR: ClarNan Editions, 1987.

- *Songs of the Classical Age*, 1990. ("Morgenlied eines armen Mannes").
- *Women's Voices: Five Centuries of Song*, 1996. ("Gärtnerliedchen aus dem Siegwart").

Zumsteeg, Emilie. "Trennung ohne Abschied." In *Frauen Komponieren: 25 Lieder für Singstimme und Klavier*, edited by Eva Rieger and Käte Walter. New York: Schott, 1992.

- Francesca Adamo Sollima. *Immagini di donna*, 2015.

Selected Secondary Sources

Appleby, David P. *The Music of Brazil*. Austin: University of Texas Press, 1983.

- Chapter 1, "Music in the Colony"
- Chapter 2, "The Braganças in Brazil"

Baker, Geoffrey and Tess Knighton, eds. *Music and Urban Society in Colonial Latin America*. Cambridge: Cambridge University Press, 2011.

- Drew Edward Davies, "Making Music, Writing Myth: Urban Guadalupan Ritual in Eighteenth-Century New Spain," 64–82.
- Paulo Castagna and Jaelson Trindade, "Chapelmasters and Musical Practice in Brazilian Cities in the Eighteenth Century," 132–50.
- Bernard Illari, "The Slave's Progress: Music as Profession in *Criollo* Buenos Aires," 186–207.

- María Gembero-Ustárroz, "Enlightened Reformism versus Jesuit Utopia: Music in the Foundation of El Carmen de Guarayos (Moxos, Bolivia), 1793–1801," 230–45.

Banat, Gabriel. "Le Chevalier de Saint-Georges, Man of Music and Gentleman-at-Arms: The Life and Times of an Eighteenth-Century Prodigy." *Black Music Research Journal* 10, no. 2 (1990): 177–212.

Cypess, Rebecca and Nancy Sinkoff, eds. *Sara Levy's World: Gender, Judaism, and the Bach Tradition in Enlightenment Berlin.* Rochester, NY: University of Rochester Press, 2018.

- Marjanne E. Goozé, "What was the Berlin Jewish Salon Around 1800?" 21–38.
- Natalie Naimark-Goldberg, "Remaining within the Fold: The Cultural and Social World of Sara Levy," 52–74. (Also applicable to the nineteenth century).

de Lerma, Dominique-René. "The Life and Works of Nunes-Garcia: A Status Report." *The Black Perspective in Music* 14, no. 2 (1986): 93–102.

DeSimone, Alison. "Musical Virtue, Professional Fortune, and Private Trauma in Eighteenth-Century Britain: A Feminist Biography of Elisabetta de Gambarini (1730–65)." *Journal of Musicological Research* 40, no. 1 (2021): 5–38.

Diedrich, Maria I. "From American Slaves to Hessian Subjects: Silenced Black Narratives of the American Revolution." In *Germany and the Black Diaspora: Points of Contact, 1250–1914*, edited by Mischa Honeck, Martin Klimke, and Anne Kuhlmann, 92–111. New York: Berghahn Books, 2013.

Head, Matthew. "Cultural Meaning for Women Composers: Charlotte ('Minna') Brandes and the Beautiful Dead in the German Enlightenment." *Journal of the American Musicological Society* 57, no. 2 (Summer 2004): 231–84.

Irving, David R.M. "The Genevan Psalter in Eighteenth-Century Indonesia and Sri Lanka." *Eighteenth-Century Music* 11, no. 2 (September 2014): 235–55.

Letzter, Jacqueline and Robert Adelson, "French Women Opera Composers and the Aesthetics of Rousseau," *Feminist Studies* 26, no. 1 (2000): 69–100.

Lindorff, Joyce. "Burney, Macartney and the Qianlong Emperor: The Role of Music in the British Embassy to China, 1792–1794." *Early Music* 41, no. 3 (2012): 441–53.

Miller, Bonny H. "Education, Entertainment, Embellishment: Music Publication in the *Lady's Magazine.*" In *Beyond Boundaries: Rethinking Music Circulation in Early Modern England*, edited by Linda Phyllis Austern, Candace Bailey, and Amanda Eubanks Winkler, 238–46. Bloomington: Indiana University Press, 2017.

Pesic, Andrei. "The Flighty Coquette Sings on Easter Sunday: Music and Religion in Saint-Domingue, 1765–1789." *French Historical Studies* 42, no. 4 (2019): 563–93.

Powers, David M. "The French Musical Theater: Maintaining Control in Caribbean Colonies in the Eighteenth Century." *Black Music Research Journal* 18, no. 1/2 (Spring–Autumn 1998): 229–40.

Prest, Julia. *"Iphigénie en Haïti:* Performing Gluck's Paris Operas in the French Colonial Caribbean." *Eighteenth-Century Music* 14, no. 1 (2017): 13–29.

Ritchie, Leslie. *Women Writing Music in Late Eighteenth-Century England: Social Harmony in Literature and Performance.* Burlington, VT: Ashgate, 2008.

- Chapter 2, "Women's Occasion for Music: The Performative Continuum & Lyrical Categories"
- Chapter 5, "Britannia; or, Women and Songs of Nation and Otherness"

Russell, Craig H. *From Serra to Sancho: Music and Pageantry in the California Missions.* New York: Oxford University Press, 2009.

- Chapter 1, "Musical Style and Performance in Mission Life"
- Chapter 3, "Serra and the Introduction of Sacred Song
- Chapter 7, "Classical Masses for Voices and Orchestra by Ignacio de Jerusalem and García Fajer"

Salwey, Nicholas. "Women Pianists in Late Eighteenth-Century London." In *Concert Life in Eighteenth-Century Britain,* edited by Susan Wollenberg and Simon McVeigh, 273–90. Burlington, VT: Ashgate, 2004.

Ustárroz, María Gembero. *"De rosas cercada:* Music by Francisco de la Huerta for the Nuns of Santa Ana de Ávila (1767–78)." In *Devotional Music in the Iberian World, 1450–1800: The Villancico and Related Genres,* edited by Knighton, Tess and Alvaro Torrente, 321–62. Burlington, VT: Ashgate, 2007.

Van der Wal, Anne Marieke. "Slave Orchestras and Rainbow Balls: Colonial Culture and Creolisation at the Cape of Good Hope, 1750–1838." In *Identity, Intertextuality, and Performance in Early Modern Song Culture,* edited by Dieuwke van der Poel, Louis Peter Grijp, and Wim van Anrooij, 352–71. Boston: Brill, 2016.

Walker, Margaret E. "The 'Nautch', the Veil and the Bayadère: The Indian Dance as Musical Nexus." In *The Music Road: Coherence and Diversity in Music from the Mediterranean to India,* edited by Reinhard Strohm, 213–35. New York: Oxford University Press, 2019.

Wheeler, Rachel and Sarah Eyerly. "Songs of the Spirit: Hymnody in the Moravian Mohican Missions." *Journal of Moravian History* 17, no. 1 (2017): 1–25.

Woodfield, Ian. *Music of the Raj: A Social and Economic History of Music in Late Eighteenth Century Anglo-Indian Society.* New York: Oxford University Press, 2000.

- Chapter 2, "Professional Musicians in India"
- Chapter 3, "The Woman Amateur"
- Chapter 5, "The Encounter with Indian Music"

Wright, Josephine R.B. "Ignatius Sancho (1729–1780), African Composer in England." *The Black Perspective in Music* 7, no. 2 (Autumn 1979): 132–67.

4   Music between 1815 and 1915

Introduction

The one hundred years between the end of Napoleon's domination of Europe (1815) and the beginning of World War I (1914) was a time of scientific advancement, the emergence of the nation state, the development of a merchant middle class, and mass migration from rural to urban areas as the working class sought employment and opportunities in the factories of the Industrial Revolution. Globalization brought about by advances in transportation, worldwide trade, and interconnected networks rooted in European colonization meant that cultural exchanges and appropriations occurred on a global scale. Some colonies gained their freedom at the beginning of the nineteenth century, but European countries continued to colonize parts of Asia, Indonesia, and Africa, a development scholars have dubbed "New Imperialism."

Classical music was the sound of nationalism and imperialism throughout the world. Colonial officials used art music to project power over their subjects. European settlers and others created elite and middle-class musical and cultural institutions in former colonies that mimicked those in Europe. People looked to culture to help define what it meant to be a citizen of a country rather than a feudal subject as monarchies fell and new nations were created. Combining influences from folk music and classical compositions written in the Austro-German style became a common way to signify nationalism in music. For people in minoritized communities, this practice could threaten their cultural heritages, or their music could be mined (even appropriated) to support patriotic projects that at once celebrated their music but denied the people who made it political power. Nineteenth-century scholars became interested in musics of Indigenous and rural or peasant cultures, although their work was often marred by biases against societies that most white people thought were inferior.

DOI: 10.4324/9781003044635-5

Economic opportunities generated by the Industrial Revolution spurred the development of the middle class and provided women and people of color with more access to music. With more disposable income to spend on it, music became a home-based, participatory, amateur activity for genteel men and women. As the century progressed, instrumental music was increasingly available to diverse audiences through public concerts. From opera companies to piano virtuosos, professional musicians undertook national and world tours that made some performers global celebrities and brought classical music to new listeners.

In Europe and the United States, women became cultural forces within their communities. Many women provided support for much of the public and private music making within their towns. They maintained respectability by directing their activities through salons, music clubs, and charitable institutions. As in the eighteenth century, salons were important spaces for musical production. The most important salon hostesses, club presidents, and patrons—Fanny Mendelssohn in Berlin, the Countess of Proença-a-Velha in Lisbon, Jeannette Thurber in New York City, Pauline Viardot in Paris to name a few—helped shape the cultural production of their cities and countries. Many of these accomplished women were professional concert organizers in all but name. A small minority of professional backstage personnel were women, including opera company music directors (Caroline Richings and Emma Abbott), publishers (Carrie Jacobs-Bond was a successful song publisher and composer), and theater managers (Lucia Elizabeth Vestris managed the Olympic, Covent Garden, and Lyceum Theatres in London). Women with enough money could easily access musical training, especially in voice and "lady-like" instruments such as violin or piano, spurring more women to become professional performers. Composition lessons were more difficult for white women to come by, although more women than ever before were able to circumvent this challenge and became active composers.

People of color participated in Western classical music, although many institutions open to white people were closed to everyone else. Some predominately white institutions and conservatories, including the Royal College of Music in London, the National Conservatory of Music in New York City, and Oberlin College in Ohio, also accepted students of color. In some cases, people of color founded parallel institutions (schools, music clubs, concert venues, performing groups, etc.) to serve their communities. In the United States, African American conductors and composers such as Frank Johnson and Joseph Postlewaite organized all-Black music groups that provided music for dances, civic, and religious celebrations. Postlewaite and James Reese Europe (a bandleader and composer) founded booking agencies to provide work for Black musicians when other organizations refused to represent them. Historically Black Colleges and Universities (HBCUs) provided African Americans with advanced training in music and used musical groups, such as the Fisk Jubilee Singers, to raise funds and awareness of Black musicianship.

The growth in professional and amateur music making resulted in a significant increase in music coverage in print media including newspapers, general interest journals, and specialized publications. They brought music education to the masses, published celebrity gossip and news, and supported music criticism and aesthetic commentary. Women and people of color participated in this print culture, especially in publications that catered to women or to a particular language/ethnic/racial group. Many ideas first pioneered by nineteenth-century music critics are still influential today such as equating excellence in classical music with "genius," and positioning art music as morally uplifting to its listeners.

Locales & Locations

Western music circulated throughout the globe—arriving with traveling virtuosos, opera companies, and instrumental groups, in sheet music bound for middle-class homes, and (at the end of the century) on piano rolls for player pianos and on recordings. Countries around the world developed cultural infrastructures and audiences to support opera houses, symphony orchestras, music halls, and musical training. European immigrants and visitors helped to establish interest in Western classical music, but local musicians and patrons sustained it, looking to European precedents for inspiration. When Brazil was a Portuguese colony, for example, classical music was largely confined to the church with a few Brazilian composers adding pieces to a mostly European repertoire. After its independence in 1822, institutions in Rio de Janeiro that supported classical music included the opera theater, concert societies, and music clubs modeled upon nineteenth-century Parisian society. As was true in other areas of the world, classical music was part of the formation of elite society. Attendance at fashionable concerts produced by musical societies supported by wealthy donors cemented a person's membership in Rio's highest socio-economic class. Brazilian amateurs and professionals provided the music, and local papers covered the performances on the society pages. Public concerts, featuring local talent and touring European professionals, linked Brazilian Imperial culture firmly to Europe through its repertoire choices and performance traditions.[1] Antônio Carlos Gomes was Brazil's most celebrated composer. His most successful opera, *Il Guarany*, premiered at La Scala in 1870. It is set in Brazil and is about the love between Cecilia, daughter of a Portuguese nobleman, and Peri, a member of the Guaraní tribe and son of its chief.[2] Gomes's music and career is one example of transnational exchange between European and non-European musicians, but it also shows the extent to which Europe often dominated these encounters. Gomes's music is in the Italian operatic style, and he chose to live in Italy rather than Brazil.

Forms & Factions

Many non-western musicians embraced art music and found ways to call the music their own, even if in some cases they replicated cultural norms that contributed to their own political marginalization. In other cases, colonial powers used music to define their nationhood culturally and, at the same time, represent their domination over Indigenous people and cultures. King George V's visit to India in late 1911 and the attendant celebrations in the colony and Great Britain is an example of this dynamic. By the middle of the nineteenth century, Great Britain directly or indirectly controlled all of India. The colony was central to British prosperity and global influence. The highlight of George V's trip to India was an elaborate ten-day celebration called the Delhi Durbar that brought together 16,000 British and twice as many Indian officials to pledge their fealty to the Emperor. Local leaders paid homage to George V and his wife, Mary, who sat on an imposing dais dressed in royal ermine. The visual components of the Durbar exoticized the Indian participants, many of whom wore traditional costumes and rode elephants, while the military uniforms of the Royal Heralds and State Trumpeters and the masculinized Western fanfares they played emphasized the power of the British Empire.[3] To mark the occasion in London, Edward Elgar collaborated with Henry Hamilton to write an "Imperial Masque" called *The Crown of India* for speakers, vocalists, and orchestra. A mix of spoken interludes and music, *The Crown of India* maintained the exoticization and feminization of India (and by implication of all colonies) while celebrating Britain's national identity and imperial ambitions. The script cast women as cities in India with texts that reflected British justifications for Indian colonization. Elgar claimed that his music contained Indian influences such as snake-charmers' pipes, "native" drums, and Indian dance music. As is often true of Romantic-era nationalism, Elgar's composition contained no authentic Indian music, but rather a jumble of musical signifiers that came out of Indian representations in English popular culture. Elgar's ambition of musically portraying India was, in reality, an exoticized and imagined perspective on the colony seen from an English nationalistic perspective.[4] In both the Durbar and Elgar's musical commemoration of it, English music controlled the sonic environment with supposedly Indian influences that only emphasized the colony's difference, foreignness, and political and cultural subordination.

Responses & Reception

Nineteenth-century music critics wielded enormous cultural capital. They shaped musical taste, and the most important critics could make or break careers. While most critics were white men, there were many people who wrote about music who were not. Music journalism existed throughout the world, and in the United States, press outlets aimed at African Americans or non-English-speaking communities hired writers from those backgrounds. Margaret Fuller (1810–50), a white woman, was one of the first Americans to write about classical music. Better known as a literary critic, Fuller became the co-editor of *The Dial* with Ralph Waldo Emerson in 1840. While at *The Dial* she gave John Sullivan Dwight (later the founder of *Dwight's Journal of Music* and the most important mid-century American music critic) his first job as a music writer. In 1844, she became the literary critic for *The New-York Tribune*. She moved to Europe in 1846 and was the first American foreign correspondent before dying in a shipwreck in 1850 on her way back to the United States. Fuller wrote extensively about the nature of beauty. Trained in music as part of the typical education for a middle-class girl, she was particularly drawn to Beethoven and attended many of the first American performances of the composer's work in New York. She published twenty-nine articles about music and described Beethoven as "towering far above our heads" with "godlike" qualities.[5] For her, the Austro-German composer was a musical genius because he created symphonic works that fulfilled what she thought of as music's unique "power to evoke a higher realm of beauty, truth, and the imagination transcending prosaic material existence."[6] According to Ora Frishberg Saloman, Fuller's enthusiastic, passionate response to Beethoven's music as a reflection of the possibility of humanity's perfection helped

> to establish the longstanding [American] public preference for the monumental Beethoven of the middle period. The writings asserted that Beethoven had opened a new era in musical style

through the communication of universal qualities with an emphasis on heroic striving and affirmation.[7]

Notes

1 See Cristina Magaldi, "Music for the Elite: Musical Societies in Imperial Rio de Janeiro," *Latin American Music Review* 16, no. 1 (Spring–Summer 1995): 1–41; and Magaldi, *Music in Imperial Rio de Janeiro: European Culture in a Tropical Milieu* (Lanham, MD: Scarecrow Press, 2004), 65–96.

2 Durval Cesetti, "*Il Guarany* for Foreigners: Colonialist Racism, Naïve Utopia, or Pleasant Entertainment?" *Latin American Music Review* 31, no. 4 (Spring–Summer 2010): 101–21; and Maria Alice Volpe, "Remaking the Brazilian Myth of National Foundation: *Il Guarany*," *Latin American Music Review* 23, no. 2 (Fall–Winter 2002): 179–94.

3 Tim Barringer, "Sonic Spectacles of Empire: The Audio-Visual Nexus, Delhi–London, 1911–12," in *Sensible Objects: Colonialism, Museums and Material Culture*, ed. Elizabeth Edwards, Chris Gosden, and Ruth B. Phillips (London: Berg Publishers, 2006), 169–94.

4 Nalini Ghuman, "Elgar and the British Raj: Can the Mughals March?" in *Edward Elgar and His World*, ed. Byron Adams (Princeton, NJ: Princeton University Press, 2007), 249–86.

5 Margaret Fuller, "Lives of the Great Composers," in *Art, Literature, and the Drama*, ed. Arthur B. Fuller (Boston: Brown, Taggard and Chase, 1860), 224, 267, quoted in Megan Marshall, "Margaret Fuller on Music's 'Everlasting Yes': A Romantic Critic in the Romantic Era," in *Margaret Fuller and Her Circles*, ed. Brigitte Bailey, Katheryn P. Viens, and Conrad Edick Wright (Durham, NH: University of New Hampshire Press, 2012), 148–60, at 154.

6 Ora Frishberg Saloman, "Margaret Fuller on Beethoven in America, 1839–1846," *Journal of Musicology* 10, no. 1 (Winter 1992): 89–105, at 93–94.

7 Saloman, "Margaret Fuller," 105.

Lesson 4.1: Harry T. Burleigh, "Through Moanin' Pines," in *From the Southland*

Background

Harry T. Burleigh (1866–1949) was among the first generation of post-slavery, Black composers who "consciously turned to the folk music of their people as a source of inspiration for their compositions," and according to Eileen Southern, he "was the first to achieve national distinction as a composer, arranger, and concert artist."[1] Burleigh's acclaim afforded collaborative opportunities with leading Black intellectuals, educators, and artists at the turn of the twentieth century.

A noted composer of art songs, ballads, and a few instrumental works, Burleigh is perhaps best known for his work with the art song spiritual. The success of his landmark arrangement of "Deep River" (1916) led to a prolific output of spiritual arrangements, some of which are standard pieces for concert performance today. A number of scholars have documented that Burleigh's professional relationship with Antonin Dvořák profoundly influenced the Czech composer's Americanist works. While working as Dvořák's copyist during his tenure at the National Conservatory of Music, Burleigh introduced the Czech composer to Black folk and plantation songs. Although Dvořák had several African American composition students during his tenure in the United States (1892–95), Burleigh was his "chief source of African American music" and "private singer of spirituals."[2] The deft combinations of African American folk forms with Western concert music defined Burleigh's prolific fifty-year career as a performer and composer.

"Through Moanin' Pines," in From the Southland (1910)

From the Southland, a set of piano sketches, is one of the three instrumental works in Burleigh's output and it is the only work for solo piano. Current analyses of the work highlight attributes of style, referring to the character of the pieces as being akin to "salon pieces, comparable in style to his [Burleigh's] light classical ballads."[3] Tuneful themes occasionally evoke a popular panache, but Burleigh also incorporates harmonic progressions more typical of late-Romantic styles that were perhaps gleaned from his familiarity with German lieder and his work with Antonin Dvořák. The suite also highlights melodic gestures suggestive of Black folk traditions as well as sprightly syncopations and quotations of preexisting tunes. Each piece is prefaced by an epigraph in Black dialect signed by Louise Alston Burleigh, though some of the lines are borrowed from pre-existing songs. Published six years before the groundbreaking "Deep River," *From the Southland* also foreshadows the neo-Romantic and modernist tenets of the succeeding generation of African American composers active during the New Negro Movement. The first sketch, "Through Moanin' Pines," is surveyed here.

Burleigh's ternary design offers a clear exposition of the main theme, harmonic and thematic contrast in the middle section, and a near literal restatement with an exploratory codetta: A (mm. 1–8), B (mm. 9–22), A (mm. 23–30), codetta (31–end). The piece is in A major, but the primary theme begins in F# minor. In fact, there is a fair amount of play between A major and F# minor in this piece. This play (or playful ambiguity) is possible, in part, because of Burleigh's choice of a pentatonic scale for the themes. The absence of mode-defining half steps in the pentatonic scale gives Burleigh enough room to experiment with relative key relationships and maintain the ethos of a vernacular thematic presence. Jean Snyder attests to the folk character of the themes, while also acknowledging their originality.[4] Amid the shift between F# minor and A major is a brief chromatic jaunt to C# major, beginning around measure 16, that provides a moment of surprise and unrest.

A closer look at the cadences and a few of Burleigh's harmonic choices unravel the tension between F# minor and A major in the primary theme. The pedal point and the cadence in measure 4 confirm F# minor as the first key center. Burleigh's modal VII-I cadence is unusual, but particularly convincing, given the anacrusis and beginning of the first phrase. The next phrase begins in F# minor, but soon and subtly migrates toward A major. The stepwise descent in the bass lands on a D in measure 6. The chord could be analyzed as ii 6/5 in A— another analysis, if based on the parallel moment in the first phrase, might be iv 6/5 in F# minor. Either analysis speaks to Burleigh's clever handling of the pentatonic melody between relative keys, but the proceeding secondary dominant-dominant-tonic progression confirms the modulation to A major and the perfect authentic cadence strengthens the arrival. The play between the relative keys becomes more vivid at the beginning of the B section (mm. 9–12) where a new thematic idea is coupled with B minor chords progressing to both F# minor and A major chords. The progression to the A major chord in m. 12 is enhanced by the chromatic shading on beat 4 of measure 11. The melodic and harmonic gestures from mm. 9–11 are essentially repeated in mm. 13–15, but the arrival on the colorful C# major chord is also a point of departure for an episode highlighting that particular harmony (mm. 16–22). Burleigh presents motivic fragments of the B section theme with dominant and Neapolitan chords (over a C# pedal) that resolve to C# major. The episode ends with an omnibus progression—where outer voices resolve outward—in measures 20–22 that eventually land on a C#7 chord, a dominant preparation for the restatement of the primary theme in F# minor.

As mentioned earlier, the return of the A section (mm. 23–30) is a near literal restatement, excepting octave doublings in the first phrase and a few chromatic, passing chords at its cadence. Following the arrival of the A major chord at the end of the second phrase (m. 30),

Burleigh restates a portion of the B section theme over an A pedal, extended/added note tertian complexes, and chromatic neighboring sonorities. The more compelling of Burleigh's harmonic choices in this codetta is the A major (add 6) chord in measure 34, as it signals a final bout of play between the key centers of F# minor and A major—both triads can be gleaned from that chord. The composer's lingering motion toward the final cadence progresses through a few more thematic fragments and a lengthier statement of the final phrase.

Locales & Locations

From his work as a soloist at St. George's Episcopal Church in Manhattan to his recital tours, Burleigh performed in concert halls, theaters, the homes of aristocrats, and a number of other traditional venues for Western concert music. His 1903 performance at the Metropolitan A.M.E Church in Washington D.C., however, is significant because of his role as soloist in the historic performance of Samuel Coleridge-Taylor's *Hiawatha's Wedding Feast*. Coleridge-Taylor was a highly respected Afro-British composer whose reputation in the United States grew, in part, through Burleigh's active promotion of his music. The Metropolitan A.M.E Church is an African American congregation and the concert consisted of "an all-black choir of one hundred sixty voices" that was assembled by the Samuel Coleridge-Taylor Choral Society.[5] Burleigh, by way of his status as a premier singer, was "the most famous of the soloists" and may have helped draw an audience that exceeded the church's seating capacity (approx. 1,800).[6] He performed to critical acclaim, garnered the respect of Coleridge-Taylor, and the two maintained a friendship until Coleridge-Taylor's death in 1912. They also shared a working relationship, as Burleigh toured with Coleridge-Taylor in each of his subsequent visits to the United States in 1904, 1906, and 1910. Coleridge-Taylor performed piano pieces from his *Twenty-Four Negro Melodies* (1905) for some of the concerts and sometimes accompanied Burleigh.[7] It is reasonable to assume that his collaborations with Coleridge-Taylor provided some inspiration for Burleigh's *From the Southland*, as the sketches are dedicated to his "friend S. Coleridge-Taylor. Esq."[8] The dedication and success of the choral society in bringing the Afro-British composer to the United States provided an opportunity for cultural uplift and pride for African Americans at the turn of the century and took place in a space that belonged to an African American congregation.

Further Consideration: Burleigh rarely traveled to the South to concertize, but he did spend some time in Georgia studying Black folk songs. This ethnographic work resulted in a co-edited hymnal published in 1929, entitled *The Old Songs Hymnal, Words and Melodies from the State of Georgia.*[9] With Dorothy Bolton as his collaborator, Burleigh traveled through rural portions of Georgia. He transcribed the tunes he heard and later prepared them for publication. We know of Burleigh as a performer and a composer, but what other motivations (cultural, personal, etc.) could there have been for this type of work?

Forms & Factions

Burleigh was among the first generation of African American composers to espouse Black nationalistic tenets in Western compositional forms—that is, the incorporation of musical emblems that signify African American culture. Such emblematic, musical signifiers of African American culture include blue notes, off-beat rhythmic emphases, call and response textures, and quotations of Black folk melodies. Although he did not formally study with Dvořák, their relationship was likely forged in part through their shared beliefs in the artistic value of folk music "and parallels in their family backgrounds."[10] Snyder notes a "deep nationalistic pride" in some of Dvořák's works that make use of Czech folk music, further claiming that "for Burleigh in particular, Dvořák's call to value and make use of the oral traditions in his own music heritage to create art music rang with transforming force."[11] The early folk ballads and instrumental works (including the aforementioned suite, *From the Southland*) demonstrate this influence. His arrangement of "Deep River" is pivotal, as that setting and subsequent settings "assumed the aesthetic values within the spiritual tradition, but reinterpreted the musical event[s] using conventions associated with the concert stage."[12] The resulting "art song spiritual" served as a point of departure for contemporaries and as a catalyst for succeeding generations of African American composers who championed the use of vernacular musical emblems.

Further Consideration: It was during the time of Burleigh's first encounters with Dvořák (the late 1890s) that many American composers were traveling to Europe to "study with masters of the German tradition."[13] Were American composers interested in an "American" sound? If they were, given the oppressive systems of race and class that were operating during that era, from where would they glean folk melodies and other elements of style that would signify an American nationalist identity? If Black composers were in search of such an identity within Western music traditions, what are some of the ways they may have navigated expectations from teachers and/or critics steeped in "Germanic" traditions?

Responses & Reception

Burleigh's reputation and accomplishment as a concert singer and his interest in preserving the folksongs of Black people likely prompted his fifteen-year relationship with Booker T. Washington, founder and first President of the Tuskegee Institute (now known as Tuskegee University, a historically Black college located in Alabama). Washington's affection for Negro folksongs extended beyond mere appreciation, as "his letters ... detailed his concern for the careful preservation and documentation of folk music and instruction of music" that he wanted at Tuskegee.[14] Burleigh traveled with and performed for Washington on a number of fund-raising trips for Tuskegee and also offered counsel on musical matters for the college. While Burleigh did not spend much time in the deep South, one could speculate that Burleigh's association with Washington at least afforded second-hand exposure to some of the dire conditions of African Americans in the Jim Crow South. In addition to increased exposure to socialites and patrons who supported Washington at select functions, Burleigh had the added benefit of "many opportunities to develop and test his art song arrangements of spirituals in the genteel milieu of the hotel and resort drawing rooms."[15] Burleigh's travels on behalf of Tuskegee continued even when Washington was unable to attend functions.[16]

   Further Consideration: Given Washington's status in the arenas of politics and education as well as Burleigh's growing prominence in the performing arts and his appointment as a hired soloist at St. George's Episcopal Church, how was their relationship mutually beneficial? There were white male composers who used musical materials from Black culture in their compositions with marginal success around the time that Burleigh began to publish his spiritual arrangements. How much of the success (critical and commercial) of his arrangements might be attributed to his race? Could the idea of authenticity have played a factor in his success and how can that idea be applied toward Burleigh's singing career which demonstrated his mastery of both Western and vernacular forms?

THROUGH MOANIN' PINES

H. T. BURLEIGH

Harry T. Burleigh, "Through Moanin' Pines," *From the Southland*

F. S.–27

Notes

1 Eileen Southern, *The Music of Black Americans: A History* (New York: Norton, 1997), 268–69.
2 Samuel A. Floyd, Jr., "The Invisibility and Fame of Harry T. Burleigh: Retrospect and Prospect," *Black Music Research Journal* 24, no. 2 (2004): 179–94, at 182.
3 Jean E. Snyder, *Harry T. Burleigh: From the Spiritual to the Harlem Renaissance* (Urbana: University of Illinois Press, 2016), 264.
4 Snyder, *Harry T. Burleigh*, 263.
5 Snyder, *Harry T. Burleigh*, 122.
6 Doris Evans McGinty, "'That You Came So Far to See Us': Coleridge-Taylor in America," *Black Music Research Journal* 21, no. 2 (Autumn 2001): 197–234, at 206–7.
7 Jeffrey Green, *Samuel Coleridge-Taylor: A Musical Life* (New York: Routledge), 133.
8 This is the dedication that appears on the score that was published in 1910.
9 Brian Moon, "Harry Burleigh as Ethnomusicologist? Transcription, Arranging, and the *Old Songs Hymnal*," *Black Music Research Journal* 24, no. 2 (2004): 287–307.
10 Snyder, *Harry T. Burleigh*, 78.
11 Snyder, *Harry T. Burleigh*, 77.
12 Olly Wilson, "Interpreting Classical Music," in *African American Music: An Introduction*, ed. Mellonee V. Burnim and Portia K. Maultsby (New York: Routledge, 2006), 230–44, at 236.
13 Snyder, *Harry T. Burleigh*, 76. Snyder compellingly refers to an essay by Nicholas E. Tawa in *Music and Culture in America, 1861–1918* (ed. Michael Saffle and James R. Heintze) that suggests that many American composers would not have chosen the music of "primitive" races as part of a "distinctly American" sound.
14 Snyder, *Harry T. Burleigh*, 120.
15 Snyder, *Harry T. Burleigh*, 121.
16 Snyder, *Harry T. Burleigh*, 125.

Lesson 4.2: African American Critical Response to Antonin Dvořák and the Problem of American Music

Background

Nineteenth-century American concert music critics and composers worried that there was no "American" musical style. Composers tried various approaches to write American art music, and critics rejected their ideas as too strange, too derivative, or too European. This seemingly straightforward task was in fact quite complex in the United States with its large immigrant population and a history of extreme oppression against Indigenous and enslaved populations. In this environment, who counted as an American? What musical tradition could be identified as "American" folk music?[1]

Douglas W. Shadle has demonstrated that composers working in the United States began wrestling with the problem of an American school of composition as early as 1800. When the United States sought to take its place as an imperial world power in the 1890s, the question of an American national style took on new urgency. Jeannette Thurber (1850–1946), a wealthy philanthropist and one of the most important cultural figures in the United States during her lifetime, entered the controversy when she brought Antonin Dvořák to New York in 1892 to be the National Conservatory of Music's second director. She founded the Conservatory in 1885 to provide professional musical training to American students including women and African Americans.[2] By building on his reputation and expertise as a Czech nationalist composer, Thurber hoped that Dvořák would spark an American musical style through his teaching and compositions. Dvořák wrote several "Americanist" works while he was in the United States including the Symphony "from the New World" which the Philharmonic Society of New York premiered at Carnegie Hall on December 16, 1893.

Dvořák touched off a new round in the American conversation on nationalist music in May 1893 when he told the *New York Herald* that

> I am now satisfied that the future music of this country must be founded upon what are called the negro melodies. This must be the real foundation of any serious and original school of composition to be developed in the United States.[3]

On the day the New World Symphony premiered Dvořák explained that in addition to "music of the negroes" he also studied "a certain number of Indian melodies" which he "tried to reproduce in my new symphony."[4] When he came to the United States, Dvořák knew little about Black music, but he learned about it from Harry Burleigh and from Mildred Hill's work on Black folk songs.[5] Although many American musicians had already concluded that Black or Native American music could be the basis of a national musical style, Dvořák's status conferred an authority on the view that no American composer could muster. Composers, critics, and other commentators weighed in on the controversy with strong opinions on all sides in a debate that lasted for many years.

Black intellectuals quickly recognized the importance of Dvořák's intervention in this national musical conversation. An article published by the *Cleveland Gazette* (a Black newspaper) on June 3, 1893 set the stage for the opinions expressed by other African American writers. The article praises Black music, connects it to slavery, and notes that this repertoire had achieved popularity in Europe and America because of touring choirs like the Fisk Jubilee Singers. The writer takes Black music out of the fields and puts into the European concert halls where he asserts it was "*the* secret of [the Jubilee choirs'] success abroad." The unnamed author declares that

> it is, as Dr. Dvorak says—if we are ever to have an American school of music—absolutely necessary that the folk songs furnished by our people while in the toils of slavery, be drawn upon for the foundation of any serious and original school of composition to be developed in this country.

Like Dvořák, the author defines Black music as spirituals created during slavery times. For Black writers, spirituals were drenched in the suffering of the enslaved, which gave the songs the moral authority to be at the center of American musical expression. In its zeal to promote Black music, however, the *Cleveland Gazette* also negated the musical heritage of Native Americans and white Americans by writing that the

> Indian has bequeathed us practically nothing in a musical line and white people have been too busy since the birth of this republic borrowing from the works of foreigners to create or originate themes upon which to build the future music of this country.

Finally, the *Cleveland Gazette* denounced racism in the United States. "The prediction that the American school of music is to be built upon what are commonly referred to as 'Negro' melodies seems to be a bitter pill indeed for many prejudiced musicians (white) to swallow."[6]

Subsequent reception of Dvořák's music and commentary about American classical music by Black writers reinforced the themes in the *Cleveland Gazette* article. Sylvester Russell was the most important African American music critic at the turn of the twentieth century. In articles in the *Freeman*, a Black newspaper from Indianapolis, Russell repeatedly evokes Dvořák's authority to bolster his claims about the significance of Black music. Russell called Dvořák "our greatest musical friend from far across the sea" and explained that when the composer praised Black music it was like a "heavy clap of thunder" to the "ears of the American white people" but that "the voice of a foreigner with superior musical knowledge resounded" in a way that no other person's opinion could.[7] He makes a direct connection between white people's acceptance of Black music as central to American nationalism and the right of African Americans to equal civil rights protections. In 1904, at the end of an essay arguing that Black music is "America's Original Music," for example, he writes "deceptive, skeptical white people of this nation will soon have to realize the truth about all the people of its nation and recognize all the rights that this country pretends to give to all."[8]

For African American writers, the stakes could not be higher. If white America could accept that Black musical production was essential to American musical identity, then the corollary must be that Black people were essential to the American nation. Historians call the years between the end of Reconstruction (1877) and 1920 the "Nadir" of American race relations because of the slow passage of Jim Crow laws that stripped African Americans of their rights and the pervasive racialized violence principally, but certainly not only, committed in the South. Many white commentators framed Black popular music—first ragtime and then jazz—as degenerate music that would corrupt white Americans; conflating similar rhetoric about Black people with their music.[9] This racist perspective affected African American writers who thought they needed to redeem Black culture in the eyes of white people in order to achieve political equality.[10] Some Black critics forcefully denounced ragtime and lauded classical music by Black composers, while others (including Russell) positioned spirituals and art music as crucial to Black musical culture but also recognized musical quality in Black popular music. In a period when increasing segregation was pushing African Americans out of the white mainstream, claiming Dvořák as an ally who centered Black music within highbrow musical compositions was a powerful argument against segregation and racial prejudice.

Today, musicologists and critics generally hear the pentatonic English horn solo in the Largo movement as resembling a spiritual and the most obvious connection to Black music in the piece. Dvořák's student William Arms Fisher used the tune in his religious folk-inspired song "Goin' Home" published in 1922. In the 1890s, however, many critics agreed with Henry Krehbiel's interpretation of the piece. He published the first review of the symphony, complete with musical examples, in the *New York Daily Tribune* on December 15, 1893. He found the "Scotch" snaps in the first movement to be representative of the vitality of the American people, and the flat seventh used in what he calls the "subsidiary melody" in the same movement to be typical of "negro music." In the second movement, he heard the haunting English horn solo as evocative of the great midwestern prairies, which brought to mind Longfellow's poem "Hiawatha."[11]

No Black critic seems to have reviewed the New World Symphony specifically, but, as shown in this essay, they certainly commented on Dvořák's ideas.

Locales & Locations

For African Americans, the history of American classical music in the nineteenth and early twentieth centuries is partly one of a constant fight against exclusion—from the concert hall, from the mainstream narrative of classical music, and from American citizenship itself. African Americans established what musicologist Naomi André calls a shadow classical music world.[12] Concerts by Black classical musicians such as Joseph Douglass (grandson of the abolitionist Frederick Douglass), Sissieretta Jones, or Sidney Woodward were held at Black churches. They performed pieces by white and Black composers including Harry Burleigh, Samuel Coleridge-Taylor, and Clarence Cameron White. Black newspapers provided a publishing outlet for Black music critics. Middle-class African Americans often thought of performing in and attending classical music concerts as an expression of "uplift"—the idea that by emulating the behavior of middle-class and wealthy white people, African Americans could dispel negative stereotypes about Black people and prove their worthiness for full citizenship rights. Dvořák's allyship presented the possibility of a bridge between Black and white musical spaces.

Further Consideration: Challenge your students to think about the classical music concerts they have attended—is the concert hall still a segregated space? Why are there so few African American classical musicians and audience members?

Forms & Factions

Looking at classical music from an alternative point of view makes it easier to see what the stakes are for non-white people in a predominately white environment. In this case, Black critics saw links between Black musical production and Black civil rights because they understood the connection between culturally derived conceptions of nationhood and the political entity of the nation. Composer Amy Beach thought that Dvořák's symphony did not "suggest their [enslaved people's] sufferings, heartbreaks" and was too "bright, cheery, and domestic."[13] She composed the *Gaelic* symphony because she believed "We of the North should be far more likely to be influenced by old English, Scotch or Irish songs inherited with our literature from our ancestors."[14] Other writers were overtly racist, such as John S. Van Cleve, who penned

> American music is a coming certainty, but it will not be made healthy by hypodermic injections of Indian or African blood. When all is said and done we are not Indians, not negroes; we are Caucasians, with blood highly complex but prevailingly Teutonic, even Saxon in its composition.[15]

What joins Beach and Van Cleve is a rejection of Black people as part of the "we" of the American nation. They could comfortably imagine different kinds of American cultural backgrounds—Beach, Irish or Scotch; Van Cleve, German—without sacrificing their sense of being Americans. Even Beach, who did not have the right to vote in the 1890s and whose career was substantially hampered by sexism, retained a strong, innate sense of American citizenship denied to a Black person.

Further Consideration: Compare the slow movements from Beach's *Gaelic* Symphony and Dvořák's New World Symphony in light of Beach's comments. Suggest students consider both pieces from a nationalistic point of view. Do either of them sound "American"? Do students agree with Beach's assessment of Dvořák's piece?

Responses & Reception

This lesson is a traditional reception study but turns to new sources outside the dominant late nineteenth-century white American critics who included Henry Krehbiel, W.J. Henderson, and Louis Elson. White critics and musicians were divided about Dvořák's advice, but for Black writers, Dvořák's promotion of Black music as fundamental to American music was a significant validation of Black culture. African American writers revered Dvořák and tried to use his ideas to leverage cultural and political citizenship for Black people. For white critics, Dvořák's ideas were provocative and potentially important, but they did not carry the cultural significance that they did for Black writers. The example of Dvořák's reception in the United States reinforces how important it is to understand the context for critical reactions to pieces of music and to gather perspectives from many different writers, not just the voices situated within the dominant power structures.

Further Consideration: Pick a recently composed piece of music (classical or otherwise) and have students find reviews from multiple sources. Help them understand the perspectives and agendas of the reviews they find.

Notes

1 Three sources that specifically address American musical nationalism and Dvořák are Michael B. Beckerman, *New Worlds of Dvořák: Searching in America for the Composer's Inner Life* (New York: Norton, 2003); Douglas W. Shadle, *Orchestrating the Nation: The Nineteenth-Century American Symphonic Enterprise* (New York: Oxford University Press, 2016); and Shadle, *Antonín Dvořák's New World Symphony* (New York: Oxford University Press, 2021). This analysis relies heavily on these sources.

2 Emanuel Rubin, "Jeannette Meyer Thurber (1850–1946): Music for a Democracy," in *Cultivating Music in America: Women Patrons and Activists since 1860*, ed. Ralph P. Locke and Cyrilla Barr (Berkeley: University of California Press, 1997), 134–59.

3 "Real Value of Negro Melodies," *New York Herald*, May 21, 1893, 28. This article was the first of seven pieces published in the *Herald* in May and June that whipped up the controversy about the subject with statements from Dvořák, European, and American composers. All articles in the *New York Herald* are available through the open-access historical newspaper database fultonhistory.com, searchable through fultonsearch.org.

4 "Dr. Dvorak's Great Symphony," *New York Herald,* December 16, 1893.

5 Jean Snyder, *Harry T. Burleigh: From the Spiritual to the Harlem Renaissance* (Urbana: University of Illinois Press, 2016), 75–90 and Beckerman, *New Worlds of Dvořák,* 84–87, 95–98.

6 All quotations from "Dr. Dvorak on the Right Track," *Cleveland Gazette*, June 3, 1893, 2. Reprinted in Lynn Abbott and Doug Seroff, *Out of Sight: The Rise of African American Popular Music, 1889–1895* (Jackson: University of Mississippi Press, 2012), 273–74.

7 Sylvester Russell, "The Great Dvorak Dead," *Freeman* (Indianapolis), June 4, 1904. The Google News Archive contains issues of the *Freeman* published between July 21, 1888, and December 25, 1915.

8 Sylvester Russell, "Music of the Slaves," *Freeman* (Indianapolis), July 30, 1904.

9 For an overview of rhetoric equating ragtime with degeneracy see Edward A. Berlin, *Ragtime: A Musical and Cultural History* (Berkeley: University of California Press, 1980), 32–44. For jazz see Maureen Anderson, "The White Reception of Jazz in America," *African American Review* 38, no. 1 (Spring 2004): 135–45.

10 Lawrence Schenbeck, *Racial Uplift and American Music, 1878–1943* (Jackson: University Press of Mississippi, 2012).

11 "Music: Dr. Dvorak's American Symphony," *New York Daily Tribune,* December 15, 1893, 7.

12 Naomi André, *Black Opera: History, Power, Engagement* (Urbana: University of Illinois Press, 2018).

13 Quoted in Sarah Gerk, "A Critical Reception History of Amy Beach's 'Gaelic' Symphony," (MA thesis, California State University, Long Beach, 2006), 19; see also Shadle, *Orchestrating the Nation*, 252.

14 "American Music," *Boston Herald*, May 28, 1893, quoted in Shadle, *Orchestrating the Nation,* 251.

15 John S. Van Cleve, "Americanism in Musical Art," *Music* 15, no. 2 (December 1898): 133.

Bibliography

Score/Recording

Orchestral

Mayer, Emilie. *Sinfonie Nr. 5, F-moll [F minor].* Edited by Cornelia Bartsch and Cordula Heymann-Wentzel. Kassel: Furore Verlag, 2005.

  • Kammersymphonie Berlin. *Emilie Mayer, Fanny Hensel, Luise Adolpha Le Beau*, 2003.

Smith, Alice Mary. *Symphonies.* Edited by Ian Graham-Jones. Middleton, WI: A-R Editions, 2003.

  • London Mozart Players. *Alice Mary Smith: Symphony in A Minor; Symphony in C Minor; Andante for Clarinet and Orchestra*, 2005.

Solo Instruments and Orchestra

Beach, Amy Marcy Cheney. *Concerto for Pianoforte and Orchestra.* Edited by Laurine Celeste Fox. Verona, NJ: Subito Music, 2017.

  • English Chamber Orchestra. *Amy Beach, Vol. 4: Empress of Night*, 2000.

Chamber Music for Winds

Farrenc, Louise. *Nonett Es-Dur [E-Flat Major]*, op. 38. Edited by Katharina Herwig. Wilhelmshaven: F. Noetzel Verlag, 2000.

  • Staatsphilharmonie Rheinland-Pfalz. *Louise Farrenc. Nonett, Es-Dur, op. 38; Sextett, c-moll, op. 40*, 2000.

Chamber Music with Piano

Coleridge-Taylor, Samuel. *Quintet in F-Sharp Minor: For Clarinet in A and String Quartet*, op. 10. Edited by Russell Denwood. Ampelforth, UK: Emerson Edition, 2010.

  • Nash Ensemble. *Coleridge-Taylor: Piano Quintet and Clarinet Quintet*, 2007.

Farrenc, Louise. *Klavierquintett Nr. 1 a-moll [A minor]*, op. 30. Edited by Katharina Herwig. Wilhelmshaven: F. Noetzel Verlag, 2001. *Klavierquintett Nr. 2 Es-Dur* [E-flat major], op. 31. Edited by Katharina Herwig. Wilhelmshaven: F. Noetzel Verlag, 2001.

  • Schubert Ensemble of London. *Louise Farrenc: The Two Piano Quintets*, 2001.

Johnson, Francis. *Bingham's Cotillion.* 1820. Library of Congress. https://www.loc.gov/resource/musm1a1.11371.0?st=gallery

  • Tami Lee Hughes. *Legacy: Violin Music of African-American Composers*, 2011.

Sonatas

Mayer, Emilie. *Sonata for Piano, D minor.* Edited by Reinhard Wulfhorst. Schwerin, Germany: Edition Massonneau, 2017.

• Yang Tai. *Emilie Mayer*, 2018.

Piano

Backer-Grøndahl, Agathe. "Trois morceaux," op. 15; "Fire Skizzer (Four Sketches)," op. 19; Prelude, op. 20, no. 1; Gavotte, op. 20, no. 3. In *Piano Music.* New York: Da Capo Press, 1982.

• *Geir Henning Braaten Plays Piano Music by Agathe Backer Grøndahl,* 2000.

Badarzewska-Baranowska, Tekla. "The Maiden's Prayer." In *Lang Lang Piano Book,* edited by Lang Lang. London: Faber Music, 2019.

• *Lang Lang Piano Book*, 2019.

Barès, Basile. *La Capricieuse: Valse,* op. 7. IMSLP. https://imslp.org/wiki/La_Capricieuse,_Op.7_(Barès,_Basile) [excerpt]

• Peter Collins. *Music of Basile Barès*, 2006.

Bomtempo, João Domingos. *Three Grand Sonatas*, op. 9. London: Clementi, Banger, et al., n.d. Sonata no. 1 in E-flat major (reprinted). In *João Domingos Bomtempo (1775–1842): obras para piano,* edited by Filipe de Sousa. Lisbon: Fundação Calouste Gulbenkian, 1980.

• Luísa Tender. *Bomtempo: Complete Piano Sonatas*, 2019.

Carreño, Teresa. *Selected Works: Piano Pieces and String Quartet.* Edited by Rosario Marciano and Carmen Rodriguez-Peralta. New York: Da Capo Press, 1984.

• Clara Rodriguez. *Carreño: Piano Music*, 2009.

Coleridge-Taylor, Samuel. *Twenty-four Negro Melodies.* Chapel Hill, NC: Hinshaw Music, 1981.

• David Shaffer-Gottschalk. *Samuel Coleridge-Taylor: 24 Negro Melodies*, 2000.

Gonzaga, Francisca "Chiquinha." "Atraente." IMSLP. https://imslp.org/wiki/Atraente_(Gonzaga%2C_Chiquinha)

• Recording and Score. YouTube: https://www.youtube.com/watch?v=o8rB0ofBYR8

Nazareth, Ernesto. "Brejiro"; "Odeon"; "Faceira"; "Apanhei-te." In *Ernesto Nazareth: para piano.* São Paulo: Irmaos Vitale, 1970.

• Marcelo Bratke. *Ernesto Nazareth: Solo Piano Works*, 2009.

Ponce, Manuel M. *Scherzino Mexicano.* New York: Peermusic, 2000.

• David Witten. *Ponce: Piano Music*, 2000.

Szymanowska, Maria. *25 Mazurkas*. Edited by Irena Poniatowska. Bryn Mawr, PA: Hildegard Publishing Company, 1993.

- Nancy Fierro. *Rags and Riches: Ragtime and Classical Piano Music by Women*, 1993.

Guitar

Holland, Justin. *Andante and Variation in C Major*. IMSLP. https://imslp.org/wiki/Andante_and_Variation_in_C_major_(Holland%2C_Justin)

- Douglas Back. *American Pioneers of the Classic Guitar: Douglas Back Plays Parlor Gems and Concert Works of William Foden (1860–1947) and Justin Holland (1819–1887)*, 1994. (listed as "An Andante")

String Quartet

Carreño, Teresa. *Streichquartett h-moll [B minor]*. Edited by Rosario Marciano. Kassel: Furore Edition, 1990.

- Carmen Rodríguez-Peralta; Arriaga String Quartet. *Teresa Carreño: Solo piano and chamber works*, 2000.

Songs

Kinkel, Johanna. *Lieder*. Vol. 1, Poetry by Geibel and Goethe. Edited by Linda Siegel. Bryn Mawr, PA: Hildegard Publishing Company, 2000.

- Ingrid Schmithüsen and Thomas Palm. *Johanna Kinkel: An Imaginary Voyage through Europe, 32 songs*, 2006. (contains 7 songs from the *Lieder,* vol. 1).

Lang, Josephine. "Mignons Klage." In *Inspired by Goethe: Songs by Women Composers of the Eighteenth and Nineteenth Centuries*, edited by Ann Willison Lemke. Kassel: Furore Verlag, 1999.

- Heike Hallaschka and Heidi Kommerell. *Josephine Lang Lieder*, 2002.

Lang, Josephine. *Selected Songs*. Edited by Judith Tick. New York: Da Capo Press, 1982.

- Heike Hallaschka and Heidi Kommerell. *Josephine Lang Lieder*, 2002.

Malibran, Maria. "Rataplan, tambour habile." In *Arie, Ariette e Romanze*, Collection I, edited by Riccardo Allorto. Milan: Ricordi, 1998.

- Cecilia Bartoli. *Maria*, 2007.

Stage

Dédé, Edmond. *Françoise et Tortillard*. IMSLP. https://imslp.org/wiki/Françoise_et_Tortillard_(Dédé%2C_Edmond)

- Hot Springs Music Festival Symphony Orchestra. *Edmond Dédé*, 2000.

Opera

Gomes, Antônio Carlos. *Il Guarany*. IMSLP. https://imslp.org/wiki/Il_Guarany_(Gomes%2C_Carlos) [full score]. Internet Archive. https://archive.org/details/ilguaranyoperaba00gome/mode/2up [piano-vocal score]

* John Neschling. *Gomes: Il Guarany*, 1996.

Joplin, Scott. *Tremonisha*. Mineola, NY: Dover Publications, 2001.

* Houston Grand Opera. Live staged recording. YouTube. https://www.youtube.com/watch?v=OLyh2jCvzG0

Viardot, Pauline. *Cendrillon*. Piano-vocal score, English translations by Rachel M. Harris. Scena Music Publishing, 2014.

* Nicholas Kok. *Cendrillon: A Chamber Operetta in Three Acts*, 2000.

Choral Works with Orchestra

Beach, Amy Marcy Cheney. *Grand Mass in E-flat Major*, op. 5. Edited by Matthew Phelps. Middleton, WI: A-R Editions, 2018.

* Stow Festival Chorus and Orchestra. *Grand Mass in E-flat Major*, 2006.

Coleridge-Taylor, Samuel. *Hiawatha's Wedding Feast*. London: Novello, 2000.

* Philharmonia Orchestra. *Samuel Coleridge-Taylor: Hiawatha's Wedding Feast, Othello Suite, Petite Suite de Concerts, and Four Characteristic Valses*, 2013.

Gomes, Antônio Carlos. *Missa de Nossa Senhora da Conceição*. IMSLP. https://imslp.org/wiki/Missa_de_Nossa_Senhora_da_Conceição_(Gomes%2C_Carlos)

* *Antônio Carlos Gomes: Missa de Nossa Senhora da Conceição*, 2005.

Silva, Francisco Manuel da. *Te deum*. IMSLP. https://imslp.org/wiki/Te_Deum_(Silva%2C_Francisco_Manuel_da)

* Coro de Câmara da Escola de Música da UFMG e orquestra. Recording. YouTube. https://www.youtube.com/watch?v=m2H8V3D8AgY

Selected Secondary Sources

Appleby, David P. *The Music of Brazil*. Austin: University of Texas Press, 1983.

* Chapter 2, "The Braganças in Brazil"

Bailey, Candace. *Music and the Southern Belle: From Accomplished Lady to Confederate Composer*. Carbondale: University of Southern Illinois Press, 2010.

* Chapter 7, "Women's Composition and Publication in the Antebellum Period"
* Chapter 9, "Confederate Women Composers"

Bashford, Christina. "Historiography and Invisible Musics: Domestic Chamber Music in Nineteenth-Century Britain." *Journal of the American Musicological Society* 63, no. 2 (2010): 291–360.

Bunzel, Anja and Natasha Loges, eds. *Musical Salon Culture in the Long Nineteenth Century.* Woodbridge: Boydell, 2019.

- Kirsten Santos Rutschman, "Fridays with Malla: Musical Repertoire in the Swedish Salon of Malla Silfverstolpe," 79–93.
- Petra Wilhelmy-Dollinger, "Traditions, Preferences and Musical Taste in the Staegemann-Olfers Salon in Nineteenth-Century Berlin," 185–97.
- Harald Krebs, "Josephine Lang and the Salon in Southern Germany," 199–210.
- Michael Uhde, "Jessie Hillebrand and Musical Life in 1870s Florence," 211–24.
- Katie A. Callam, "An Invitation to 309 Beacon Street: Clara Kathleen Rogers and her Boston Salon," 225–38.

Chybowski, Julia J. "Becoming the 'Black Swan' in Mid-Nineteenth-Century America: Elizabeth Taylor Greenfield's Early Life and Debut Concert Tour." *Journal of the American Musicological Society* 67, no. 1 (2014): 125–65.

Clark, Walter A. "The Philippines, Latin America, and Spain." In *Nineteenth-Century Choral Music*, edited by Donna M. Di Grazia. 449–71. New York: Routledge, 2013.

de Lerma, Dominique-René. "Black Composers in Europe: A Works List." *Black Music Research Journal* 10, no. 2 (1990): 275–334.

Floyd, Samuel A. "A Black Composer in Nineteenth-Century St. Louis." *19th-Century Music* 4, no. 2 (Autumn 1980): 121–33.

Friedland, Bea. *Louise Farrenc, 1804–1875: Composer, Performer, Scholar.* Ann Arbor, MI: UMI Research Press, 1980.

- Chapter 8, "Piano Music"
- Chapter 9, "Chamber Music"
- Chapter 10, "Orchestral Music"

Green, Jeffrey, ed. Special Issue on Samuel Coleridge-Taylor. *Black Music Research Journal* 21, no. 2 (Autumn 2001).

- Catherine Carr, "From Student to Composer: The Chamber Works," 179–96.
- Paul Richards, "A Pan-African Composer? Coleridge-Taylor and Africa," 235–60.
- Geoffrey Self, "Coleridge-Taylor and the Orchestra," 261–82.

Gross, Klaus-Dieter. "The Politics of Scott Joplin's *Treemonisha*." *Amerikastudien / American Studies* 45, no. 3 (2000): 387–404.

Howe, Sondra Wieland. "The Role of Women in the Introduction of Western Music in Japan." *The Bulletin of Historical Research in Music Education* 16, no. 2 (January 1995): 81–97.

Kenny, Aisling and Susan Wollenberg, eds. *Women and the Nineteenth-Century Lied.* Burlington, VT: Ashgate, 2015.

- Chapters on Pauline von Decker, Fanny Hensel, Clara Schumann, Josephine Lang, Pauline Viardot, Ethel Smythe and Alma Mahler

König, José Manuel Izquierdo. "Rossinian Opera in Translation: José Bernardo Alzedo's Church Music in Mid-Nineteenth-Century Chile." *The Opera Quarterly* 35, no. 4 (2019): 251–75.

MacLeod, Beth Abelson. *Fannie Bloomfield-Zeisler: The Life and Times of a Piano Virtuoso.* Urbana: University of Illinois Press, 2015.

* Chapter 4, "Establishing a Career"
* Chapter 5, "On Tour before Domestic Audiences"

Newark, Cormac, ed. *The Oxford Handbook of the Operatic Canon.* New York: Oxford University Press, 2020.

* Benjamin Walton, "Canons of Real and Imagined Opera: Buenos Aires and Montevideo, 1810–1860," 271–91.
* Hilary Poriss, "Redefining the Standard: Pauline Viardot and Gluck's *Orphée*," 361–81.

Olwage, Grant. "John Knox Bokwe, Colonial Composer: Tales about Race and Music." *Journal of the Royal Musical Association* 131, no. 1 (2006): 1–37.

Porter, Cecelia Hopkins. *Five Lives in Music: Women Performers, Composers, and Impresarios from the Baroque to the Present.* Urbana: University of Illinois Press, 2012.

* Chapter 3, "Josephine Lang: The Music of Romanticism in South German Cultural Life"

Sears, Ann. "'A Certain Strangeness': Harry T. Burleigh's Art Songs and Spiritual Arrangements." *Black Music Research Journal* 24, no. 2 (Autumn 2004): 227–49.

Southern, Eileen. "Frank Johnson of Philadelphia and His Promenade Concerts." *The Black Perspective in Music* 5, no. 1 (1977): 3–29.

Thurman, Kira. "Black Venus, White Bayreuth: Race, Sexuality, and the Depoliticization of Wagner in Postwar West Germany." *German Studies Review* 35, no. 3 (October 2012): 607–26.

Velásquez, Juan Fernando. "From the *Plaza* to the *Parque*: Transformations of Urban Public Spaces, Disciplining, and Cultures of Listening and Sound in Colombian Cities (1886–1930)." *Latin American Music Review* 38, no. 2 (Fall–Winter 2017): 150–84.

Weber, William, ed. *The Musician as Entrepreneur, 1700–1914: Managers, Charlatans, and Idealists.* Bloomington: Indiana University Press, 2004.

* Paula Gillett, "Entrepreneurial Women Musicians in Britain: From the 1790s to the Early 1900s," 198–220.
* Jann Pasler, "Countess Greffulhe as Entrepreneur: Negotiating Class, Gender, and Nation," 221–49.

Wright, Josephine. "*Das Negertrio* Jimenez in Europe." *The Black Perspective in Music* 9, no. 2 (Autumn 1981): 161–76.

Wyatt, Lucius R. "Six Composers of Nineteenth-Century New Orleans." *Black Music Research Journal* 10, no. 1 (1990): 125–40.

Xepapadako, Avra. "European Itinerant Opera and Operetta Companies Touring in the Near and Middle East." In *The Music Road: Coherence and Diversity in Music from the Mediterranean to India*, edited by Reinhard Strohm. 319–37. New York: Oxford University Press, 2019.

5 Music after 1915

Introduction

The twentieth and twenty-first centuries have been marked by global up-
heaval and confrontations—two world wars, the Great Depression of the
1930s, the Cold War of the mid-twentieth century, and the global pandemic to name but a few. These difficult years seemed to spur composers
to a new determination to innovate within a Western classical musical
style still closely associated with the old world of European aristocracy.
Eager to be part of the avant-garde, composers followed multiple musical
paths resulting in the stylistic variation that is the hallmark of modern
music. Although classical music is an entrenched part of elite cultures all
over the world, it was, and still is, most closely associated with whiteness,
wealth, and the imperialism of the United States and Europe.

In the nineteenth century, nationalist music was usually understood
by composers as a way to glorify newly emerging nation-states, but in
the twentieth century, the idea of nationalism became more nuanced,
as composers and performers struggled to define their subject position
within their countries. For some composers of color, the marriage of
techniques from classical music with those found in vernacular musical traditions from their cultural/racial/ethnic backgrounds was
(and is) a way to carve out a space for themselves in the art music
establishment and demonstrate their skill and pride to members of
the dominant culture. Others also understand their compositions as
resistance against harmful stereotypes and the consequences of colonization. For example, Louis Ballard, a Quapaw/Cherokee composer
from the United States, positioned his music as re-invigorating Western classical music by unifying those traditions with musical elements
drawn from various Native musics.[1] This orientation is in keeping with
Indigenous beliefs that center harmony and communitarianism while
fighting the legacy of settler colonialism.[2]

DOI: 10.4324/9781003044635-6

The troubling connections between colonialism and classical music have not meant that former colonies have abandoned classical music. South Africa, for instance, has a thriving opera scene that dates back to the British occupation. In the post-apartheid era, Black singers and composers have moved into mainstream South African operatic establishments, collaborating with white musicians to produce European classics and new works. Bongani Ndodana-Breen's score for *Winnie: The Opera* (2011), an operatic treatment of the life of Winnie Madikizela-Mandela, integrates traditional African music with European classical music. Although the work requires musicians trained in Western art music, the score also calls for South African instruments alongside the standard European orchestra, and the libretto mixes English and isiXhosa. Naomi André argues that Black South African composers use opera as a method of defining their nation's cultural identity in much the same way that Europeans have done for centuries.[3]

The institutions and cultural practices that provided women with access to power as salon hostesses, patrons, and leaders of music clubs began to deteriorate by the mid-twentieth century. Before that happened, American Black and white women promoted musical culture through music clubs, and individuals (such as Elizabeth Sprague Coolidge) poured their wealth into supporting organizations and musicians. The women's auxiliaries of orchestras and opera companies provided free labor for fundraising, while allowing women a socially acceptable way of wielding public influence. Although few women composers were programmed by major groups, they were supported by women's organizations that routinely programmed their music in recitals and sponsored educational events that spotlighted women's music.[4] Today, much of the work done by volunteers before World War II is now handled by professionals. As is true of other industries, white women and people of color are underrepresented in top positions in arts management and major philanthropic institutions that support classical music, though there are obvious exceptions such as Eva Wagner-Pasquier and Katharina Wagner, the managers of the Bayreuth Festival, Kathryn McDowell, the managing director of the London Symphony Orchestra, and Robert F. Smith who became the first African American chairman of Carnegie Hall's Board of Trustees in 2016.

Despite efforts to diversify classical music, white women and people of color still face systemic and cultural challenges to their participation in every facet of art music. A report on American orchestras in 2016 found that just 1.8% of symphony members were Black.[5] The number of white women in US orchestras is higher following a systemic change. A 1997 study found that after American orchestras implemented blind auditions in the 1970s, the share of women members in the top five orchestras rose from less than 5% to 25%.[6] Conductors are also still virtually all male and all white. In 2014, only 1.4% of the people employed to conduct British orchestra were women.[7] The Metropolitan Opera went one hundred years between performances of an opera by a woman (Ethel Smyth in 1903 to Kaija Saariaho in 2016) and did not mount an opera by a Black composer until 2021.[8] The use of blackface by white singers performing Black roles is a particularly offensive practice that still exists in opera. Russian-born soprano Anna Netrebko, for example, has refused to stop darkening her skin when singing the title role in *Aida,* despite numerous calls for her to end the practice.

There are many people who are advocating for widespread changes in the classical music industry to protect people from exploitation and harassment and to overturn policies that have perpetuated the structures that impede white women and people of color.[9] Groups such as the Chineke! Orchestra (a majority-Black orchestra in the United Kingdom) provide employment and support for musicians of color in myriad ways.[10] Some major organizations have responded to pressures to de-emphasize canonic compositions in the performing repertoire by launching initiatives to promote composers from underrepresented groups, such as the New York Philharmonic's Project 19 that commissioned new pieces from nineteen women composers.[11] Yet many challenges remain to dislodge the hold that the canon has on classical music. In an analysis of the repertoire programmed by 120 American orchestras in the 2019–20 season, 8% of the pieces were by women composers, while 12.5% of the compositions were by Beethoven.[12]

Locales & Locations

The connections between European and American high culture, modernity, and political power are as important in the twentieth and twenty-first centuries as they were in earlier eras. Even countries politically aligned against the West are still drawn to classical music for artistic and economic reasons. As local political conditions change, however, the role of classical music also shifts. The history of Western classical music in China, for example, stretches back to the early seventeenth century when the emperor received a clavichord from a visiting Jesuit. Eager to position the city as the "Paris of the East," leaders in Shanghai began trying to host an orchestra in the late nineteenth century, but it was not until 1919 that the Shanghai Municipal Orchestra was born, under the direction of Mario Pacio (an Italian), staffed by non-Chinese musicians, with few Chinese people even allowed to attend concerts. The orchestra was part of an outward-facing Westernization, designed to appeal to foreign visitors and investors. Later, Communist officials, inspired by the importance of the arts in the USSR, promoted Chinese-influenced classical music by Chinese composers such as Ma Ke and Xian Xinghai alongside traditional Chinese arts. The rejection of all things Western during the Cultural Revolution resulted in the denunciation, imprisonment, and deaths of classical musicians, but Jiang Qing (Mao Zedong's powerful wife), turned to music and theater to "revolutionize" the country. She began to encourage classical music with approved political content that was heavily influenced by Chinese traditions and written by Chinese composers in the late 1960s. In the early 1970s, Premier Zhou Enlai used the performance of Western art music as a signal to European and American leaders of his desire to re-engage with the West. The Central Conservatory enrolled its first class after the Cultural Revolution in 1978, and by 1983 had invited over one thousand foreign musicians to work with their students, creating a rich site of cultural exchange. In an example of the transnational and global nature of art music, three graduates of that first class, Chen Yi, Zhou Long (both Pulitzer Prize winners), and Tan Dun now live and work in the United States. Today, municipal Chinese governments and national leaders take advantage of classical music's link to Western-style modernity to frame China as progressive, forward-leaning, and eager for contacts with Europe and America.[13]

Forms & Factions

Composers, performers, and others have recruited classical music into political work throughout the Modern Era. Joel Thompson's "Seven Last Words of the Unarmed" (2015), modeled on Joseph Haydn's "The Seven Last Words of Our Savior on the Cross," for instance, sets the final utterances of seven African American men killed by the police or other authority figures, dramatizing the white supremacist violence and police brutality that animates the Black Lives Matter Movement.[14] The case of Silvestre Revueltas (1899–1940) is another example of a composer whose artistic activities were entangled with his political beliefs. A composer, violinist, and conductor, Revueltas was a political Leftist and a Mexican nationalist. Along with Carlos Chávez, he was one of the most important nationalist composers in Mexico. He taught violin and composition and conducted the orchestra at the National Conservatory. Peter Garland describes Revueltas's use of Indigenous Mexican music in his modernist compositions as similar to that of a Cubist artist who "takes this tradition and rhythmically breaks it up ... motivic pieces are perceived like fragments in a painting: violins playing a melody in thirds here; a lone trumpet there..."[15] In line with Stalinist cultural ideology, Revueltas did not recognize class-based differences in music and thought that "music, life and revolution (social and artistic) were not separable."[16] At the height of the Spanish Civil War in 1937, he traveled to Spain to conduct his music. Revueltas, along with the Mexican government, was a strong supporter of the Spanish Republicans, seeing their cause as an extension of the Mexican Revolution of 1910. Throughout the tour, he and the Spanish press framed his presence in the country as a gesture of political solidarity with Republicans, and his music as populist and a reflection of a "revolutionary" aesthetic.[17]

Responses & Reception

Critical and industry reception of non-white classical musicians has resulted in the amplification of a few individuals while at the same time suppressing the true extent of participation in art music by white women in atypical roles (such as conductor) and people of color. For example, contralto Marian Anderson was one of many Black operatic singers in the first half of the twentieth century. For a time, she was one of the most famous western art singers in the world. Yet, paradoxically, her fame overshadowed the careers of other Black singers of the period such as Caterina Jarboro, Jules Bledsoe, or Lillian Evanti. Often tokenized in life, Anderson has suffered historical tokenism as well. While some Black vocalists have forged successful international singing careers, they have never been able to sing the range of roles or take advantage of the scope of opportunities afforded white singers of similar caliber. As was true of Anderson and tenor Roland Hayes, many Black American opera singers and classical musicians went to Europe during the first half of the twentieth century to find more opportunities to perform and to receive advanced training. While Black musicians in Europe (whether born there or émigrés) found a more hospitable environment in Europe than in America, they were still subject to racial prejudice which affected their reception by critics and audiences as well as their employment opportunities.[18]

Notes

1　Tara C. Browner, "Transposing Cultures: The Appropriation of Native North American Musics, 1890–1990," (Ph.D. diss., University of Michigan, 1995), 169–70.

2 Dawn Ierihó:Kwats Avery, "Native Classical Music: *Non:wa* (Now)," in *Music and Modernity Among First Peoples of North America*, ed. Victoria Lindsay Levine and Dylan Robinson (Middletown, CT: Wesleyan University Press, 2019), 198–219, at 201.

3 Naomi André, "*Winnie*, Opera, and South African Artistic Nationhood," *African Studies* 75, no. 1 (2016): 10–31.

4 For one example see Marian Wilson Kimber, "Grace Porterfield Polk and the American Song Composers' Festival," *Women's Song Forum*, January 16, 2021, https://www.womensongforum.org/2021/01/16/grace-porterfield-polk-and-the-american-song-composers-festival/.

5 League of American Orchestras, "Racial/Ethnic and Gender Diversity in the Orchestra Field," September 2016, 3, http://www.ppv.issuelab.org/resources/25840/25840.pdf.

6 Claudia Goldin and Cecilia Rouse, "Orchestrating Impartiality: The Impact of 'Blind' Auditions on Female Musicians," NBER Working Paper No. 5903, issued January 1997.

7 Farah Nayeri, "When an Orchestra Was No Place for a Woman," *New York Times*, December 23, 2019, https://www.nytimes.com/2019/12/23/arts/music/women-vienna-philharmonic.html

8 In September 2019, the Metropolitan Opera announced they would produce Terence Blanchard's *Fire Shut Up in My Bones* during the 2020–21 season; however, with the organization's schedule upended by the COVID-19 pandemic, the work did not premiere until the opening night of the following season on September 27, 2021.

9 Examples of organizations dedicated to this goal range from Castle of Our Skins, a concert and educational organization, to scholarly groups such as the Black Opera Research Network.

10 Chineke! Foundation, https://www.chineke.org/

11 Project 19, *New York Philharmonic*, https://nyphil.org/concerts-tickets/explore/project-19

12 Data Analysis of Orchestral Seasons 2019–20, *Institute of Composer Diversity*, https://www.composerdiversity.com/orchestra-seasons. For an explanation of the systemic barriers to programming music outside of the canon, see Douglas Shadle, "Systemic Discrimination: The Burden of Sameness in American Orchestras," *I Care If You Listen*, February 8, 2018, https://www.icareifyoulisten.com/2018/02/systemic-discrimination-burden-sameness-american-orchestras/

13 This paragraph is based upon Sheila Melvin and Jindong Cai, *Rhapsody in Red: How Western Classical Music Became Chinese* (New York: Algora Publishing, 2004).

14 See https://sevenlastwords.org/ on Thompson's composition.

15 Peter Garland, *In Search of Silvestre Revueltas: Essays 1978–1990* (Santa Fe: Soundings Press, 1991), 164–65.

16 Garland, *In Search of Silvestre Revueltas*, 152.

17 Carol A. Hess, "Silvestre Revueltas in Republican Spain: Music as Political Utterance," *Latin American Music Review/Revista de Música Latinoamericana* 18, no. 2 (Autumn–Winter, 1997): 278–96.

18 Kira Thurman, *Singing Like Germans: Black Musicians in the Land of Bach, Beethoven, and Brahms* (Ithaca, NY: Cornell University Press, 2021).

Lesson 5.1: Chou Wen-chung, Suite for Harp and Wind Quintet

Background

Composer, pedagogue, and cultural ambassador Chou Wen-chung (1923–2019) has a distinctive compositional voice that resonates with deference to both Eastern influences and Western traditions. Born in China, he was exposed to traditional Chinese music as well as the music of the classical tradition during his younger years. Although he pursued advanced studies in science as a young adult, earning a degree in civil engineering in 1945, Chou's continued and deep engagement with music led him to the United States to pursue his education at the New England Conservatory in 1946.[1] Following a move to New York, his interests in composition were enriched through mentoring from Edgard Varèse; their relationship extended beyond that of teacher/student, becoming a friendship that lasted until Varèse's death in 1965. As his compositional voice developed during the middle decades of the twentieth century, Chou's artistic philosophy of "re-merger" began to take root in his aesthetic choices and compositional processes. Ultimately he viewed Eastern and Western music as originating from the "same sources," "the fusion of Eastern and Western elements in music is a 'reunion' after centuries of divergence."[2] Chou became a naturalized citizen of the United States and landed his first academic post in 1958.[3] He went on to hold teaching and administrative appointments at several universities, including Columbia University, while also curating Varèse's estate and working with the Center for U.S.-China Arts Exchange. He earned a number of commissions and honors, and his output includes works for various ensembles and performance mediums, including incidental music.

An Excerpt from Suite for Harp and Wind Quintet (1951)

Chou's *Suite for Harp and Wind Quintet* sits among a few works composed at the beginning of his career. This early period, as explained by Eric Lai, is characterized by pieces that involve "Chou's earliest attempt to incorporate Chinese elements within the framework of Western composition" by way of "the quotation of Chinese pentatonic melodies."[4] Whereas some early works borrow directly from traditional melodies, behaving more like "arrangements" of tunes, others incorporate a "freer" borrowing of source material that is subject to contemporary treatments such as "fragments with unconventional modulations."[5] Such treatments exemplify Chou's initial aesthetic in regard to Western compositional techniques as he aimed "to recapture the color, mood and emotion implied in the seemingly simple folk material, by means of its own transmutation without adding whatsoever that is not aurally present in itself."[6] The resulting soundscape in the Suite features sudden changes in texture, tonal centers, and timbres, as intervallic relationships within the melody "generate" structural attributes such as form, harmony, and rhythm. To that end, composer and critic Lester Trimble noted a "pointillist manner" in Chou's treatment of melody, lauding "a wealth of harmonic and instrumental color without losing the essential character" of the five traditional Chinese melodies on which the piece is based.[7]

Chou's *Suite* comprises five movements that are performed without a break. The movement's boundaries are denoted with double bars and tempo/performance markings, such as "Moderato tranquillo," found at the beginning of the first movement (mm. 1–42) which is the excerpt of our focus. Pentatonicism is paramount in this movement, as melodic and harmonic constructs are derived primarily from anhemitonic pentatonic scales—five-note scales that do not contain half steps. The pitch collections employed are of the major pentatonic type, although the "tonic" notes sometimes differ from traditional realizations of that scale. Frequent modulations and compellingly textured transitional episodes render a modern technique as well as idiomatic gestures that, at times, signal inspiration from Chinese culture. While not in a mirror form, Chou's arch shape is framed by melodic fragments in f minor (mm. 1–4 and 37–42) and expressively marked with a solo phrase in the harp in the middle of movement (mm. 19–21). Figure 5.1 provides the traditional melody from which the material for this movement is derived. The A and B phrase markings denote the fragments that Chou develops throughout the movement.[8] In following Chou's formal trajectory for this movement, the three subsections are based on the beginnings of melodic statements: Section I (mm. 1–16), Section II (mm.17–27), and Section III (mm. 28–42).

The first four measures of the *Suite* foreshadow the melodic utterances, pentatonic pitch structures, and pointillistic textures that characterize much of the first movement's content. Measures 1 and 2 expose a precursory, pointillistic gesture that introduces all the instruments in the wind quintet, doubled by the harp. The four pitches sound in this introductory gesture (F, A*b*, B*b*, and E*b*) comprise the first four notes of the Fragment *a*. A more linear realization of Fragment *a* continues

Figure 5.1 Traditional Chinese melody, adapted by Eric C. Lai.

in measure 3. It appears Chou is hinting toward an A♭ pentatonic collection, and it is confirmed when C arrives at the end of measure 4.[9] Considering the prevalence of F in the bass in these opening measures, we refer to this brief passage as being in F minor. A similar precursory gesture (mm. 5–6) serves as a transition to a longer melodic statement shared between the oboe and clarinet (from Fragment *a*; mm. 7–10). Transposed to a B♭ major collection, it is also important to note Chou's technique here, as "certain melodic intervals within a phrase [are] assigned to different registers on particular instruments to achieve the sonorities and colors that are already implied by the melody itself."[10] This particular treatment is pointillistic to a degree but is more reminiscent of *Klangfarbenmelodie*.[11] An abrupt modulation to an A major collection occurs in measures 11 through 16, as Fragment *b* ensues, shared between flute, oboe, clarinet, and horn. The harp serves as an accompanimental voice throughout this section, adding harmonic underpinnings for F# minor (the relative minor of A major) in measures 11–16.

Section II begins with another two-measure, precursory episode introducing the pitch content of the first measure of Fragment *a* and is followed by a more linear realization in the harp, all featuring an E♭ major collection. The statement by the harp beginning in measure 19 is structurally significant because it is the only one in this movement that is not shared, and because it affords the opportunity to hear the melody unshared. That Chou utilizes the harp in this way is compelling, as the timbral contrast yields a color not experienced up to this point and, perhaps, suggests an idiomatic reference to a traditional Chinese string instrument. An abrupt modulation to an E major collection occurs immediately in measure 23, as another statement of Fragment *b* begins. Whereas the prior occurrence of this fragment rested squarely in F# minor, this statement, shared between the bassoon, horn, and clarinet, loosely hints toward E major because of the initial gesture in measures 22–23. The lack of strong melodic closure in C# caused by the pointillistic articulations in the winds and the low F# in the harp (mm. 26–27), however, point to a more complex realization of Chou's fragmentation technique and his favoring of color and affect over sectional rigidity. Measures 26–27, therefore, function both as a moment of closure for the abbreviated melody and also as an intra-musical reference to the precursory gesture that signals the beginning of a new idea.

New tremolo figures presented in each wind instrument (mm. 28–31) mark the beginning of Section III. The figures serve as a harmonic accompaniment for leaping harp motifs which perpetuate the pervasive linear character of the movement. Chou presents these figures at two pitch levels—C major and D major, respectively. At the conclusion of the D major figure (m. 31), Fragment *a* ensues in the same key. The significance of this statement lies within its instrumentation: it is the only fragment shared between each wind instrument. Harp glissandi (based on D major pentatonic) at the conclusion of that statement are interrupted by an E*b* and F-natural in the horn (mm. 34–35). These pitches prepare the upcoming precursory gesture and concluding, framing figure in F minor, but they also comprise the most chromatic moment in the piece. Chou's modulations visit many different keys over the course of the first movement, but each visit primarily employs pitches from pentatonic scales—whether the modal implications are major or minor. Therefore, the semitone dissonances created by the E*b* and F against the D major pentatonic scale subtly and expressively direct the listener to a colorful shift in texture that prepares a concluding episode and an abbreviated utterance of a portion Fragment *a* (mm. 40–42).

Locales & Locations

Chou began studying with the French ultra-modernist composer Edgard Varèse in 1949, sharing portions of *Landscapes* with his teacher in an early lesson. To Chou's surprise, Varèse liked the score and asked Chou to return for another lesson. The apprenticeship lasted for five years, and their friendship endured until Varèse's death in 1965. Chou "began to find his compositional voice" through Varèse's encouragement "of an intrinsic style, one that takes root in the persona of the composer" and a "mantra" that insists that "you have to find your own way."[12] Such pursuits led Chou back to his birthplace to study classical Chinese music, as well as other Chinese arts and poetry, during the mid-to-late 1950s. Select works from the periods of study with Varèse and in China actively engaged elements from Chinese culture, proving to be "indicators of the compositional direction that Chou would pursue during the course of his career" and "decisive in the progress of his career."[13] For example, the 1958 recording of *Landscapes* was his first professional recording and the 1961 recording of *And the Fallen Petals* by the Louisville Orchestra was part of a commission.

Further Consideration: Chou, a long-time friend of the Varèse family, maintained and curated Varèse's "musical estate" dating back to 1963.[14] What types of lessons and/or values might have Chou gleaned from his teacher's appreciation, collecting, and study of early music and composers?

Forms & Factions

Chou founded the Center for U.S.-China Arts Exchange in 1978. Its mission involved the promotion and enabling of exchanges among visual artists, performing artists, and literary figures between the two countries. Through the sponsorship of agencies such as the Ford Foundation, research grants, and institutional support (including Columbia University), this organization worked to foster collaborative endeavors that provided engaging programming for audiences. Biographer Mark Radice positions Chou's founding of the Exchange as

> a pivotal moment in the political and cultural history of the People's Republic of China. The devastation of the arts that took place during Mao Zedong's regime deprived Chinese artists of the opportunity to study Western music for decades.[15]

Although met with some political challenges brought about by diplomats in both countries, the Exchange was successful in fulfilling its mission not only from the standpoint of artists' visiting and sharing in various venues in the two countries, but also in raising awareness of the richness of Asian artistic culture in the West. As Chinese musicians began to study and perform Western music again, they were also encouraged to value and embrace their heritage. Chou's aesthetic of the merging of the East and West in his compositional voice expanded beyond the concert hall and found fertile ground in the Center's expansive and complex efforts.

Further Consideration: The Center's extensions in both geography and disciplinary focus demonstrate an almost humanitarian assignment that reaches beyond the initial imperatives of Chou's mission. As the Center could be viewed as Chou's reaction to the artistic voids he noticed in his homeland, discuss ways that musical organizations/societies/ensembles can collaborate with other arts disciplines to affect societal change? In which ways could music (traditional or Western music) aid humanitarian agendas, locally or abroad?

Responses & Reception

Mark Steinberg's illuminating essay "Chou as Composer and Collaborator" offers first-hand accounts of how Chou and the Brentano String Quartet worked together toward the premiere performances of the first and second string quartets.[16] Chou was demanding in some ways, but also sensitive to the ears and the musical aptitude of the performers. For the first quartet, Steinberg mentioned the frustration that arose because the ensemble's sound did not match the color Chou wanted for a particular pizzicato passage. The ensemble decided to use guitar picks to get close to the sound of a traditional Chinese instrument and Chou approved the change.[17] His trust in the musicianship of the Brentano Quartet was most evident when Chou solicited input and suggestions for the first quartet. Although they initially were reluctant to give advice, Chou considered their suggestions for the end of the work and made the changes they recommended. Steinberg's gracious recollections likely stemmed from "the evolution of the piece that came from the interaction between the composer and the performer" and an involvement that allows one to "feel like the piece almost tailor-made for you, or that you can tailor yourself to the piece."[18] String Quartet no. 1, "Clouds," was completed and premiered in 1996.

Further Consideration: Considering the moments of frustration or disconnect between the composer, performers, and the score in the "pizzicato" passage, discuss the potential advantages and disadvantages of having the composer be a part of the rehearsal/preparation process. Are these potential issues only applicable to classical music where there is a notable distance between composer, performer, and audience?

SUITE
FOR HARP AND WIND QUINTET

CHOU WEN-CHUNG

*) Harmonics are written where they actually sound.
**) To let vibrate.

Edition Peters 6205

*) Muffle the given notes with the fingers.
Edition Peters 6205

*) With the flat of the hand, muffle simultaneously the given notes
and all those in between.

Edition Peters 6205

Notes

1 Eric C. Lai, *The Music of Chou Wen-chung*, (Burlington, VT: Ashgate, 2009), 8.
2 Lai, *Music of Chou Wen-chung*, 14.
3 Mark A. Radice, "Chou Wen-chung: A Biographical Essay," in *Polycultural Synthesis in the Music of Chou Wen-chung*, ed. Mary I. Arlin and Mark A. Radice (New York: Routledge, 2018), 17–85, at 39.
4 Lai, *Music of Chou Wen-chung*, 23.
5 Lai, *Music of Chou Wen-chung*, 23.
6 Introduction to *Suite for Harp and Wind Quintet,* Chou Wen-chung website, https://chouwenchung.org/composition/suite-for-harp-and-wind-quintet/
7 Chou Wen-Chung, *Suite for Harp and Wind Quintet* (New York: C.F. Peters, 1962), inside front cover.
8 Eric Lai, "Musical Brushstrokes: Calligraphy and Texture in Chou Wen-chung's Music," in *Polycultural Synthesis in the Music of Chou Wen-chung*, ed. Mary I. Arlin and Mark A. Radice (New York: Routledge, 2018), 86–121, at 93. Many thanks to Eric Lai for discussing the attributes of this traditional melody. This example is an adaptation of a melodic reduction created by Eric Lai who states that this melody was also used in Chou's orchestral work *Landscapes* (1949).
9 We note here that Chou's score is a transposed score.
10 Introduction to *Suite for Harp and Wind Quintet.*
11 Lai, *Music of Chou Wen-chung*, 108. Lai mentions this type of melodic treatment in discussing Chou's early approaches to texture and timbre.
12 Radice, "Biographical Essay," 28.
13 Radice, "Biographical Essay," 32.
14 Radice, "Biographical Essay," 61.
15 Radice, "Biographical Essay," 57.
16 Mark Steinberg, "Snapshot: Chou as Composer and Collaborator," in *Polycultural Synthesis in the Music of Chou Wen-chung*, ed. Mary I. Arlin and Mark A. Radice (New York: Routledge, 2018), 215–16.
17 Steinberg, "Chou as Composer," 213.
18 Steinberg, "Chou as Composer," 214.

Lesson 5.2: American Nationalism: Florence Price in Counterpoint with Aaron Copland

Background

During the 1930s, a group of African American composers wrote music that was conservative in form and harmonic language. William Dawson, William Grant Still, and Florence Price were all successful at the time: major orchestras premiered a symphony each composed, and they all were influenced by spirituals and other forms of Black music.

At the same time, some white American composers including Aaron Copland, Roy Harris, and Virgil Thomson developed what Richard Taruskin calls an American pastoral style that valued simplicity, drew from Stravinskian neo-classicism, and pushed against the complexity and dissonance of the musical avant-garde.[1] All of these composers reflected facets of American national identity in their work—but whose America? And what conception of Americanness did they depict? This lesson pairs the third movement, "Juba Dance" from Florence Price's Symphony in E minor (1933) with Aaron Copland's "Hoe-Down" from *Rodeo* (1942). The goal is to interrogate different visions of American nationalism, whose conceptions of Americanness were and are valued, and how these two composers incorporated vernacular influences into their concert music.

Florence Price wrote in an accessible style that often married Black vernacular music with the techniques of western classical music. Born in Little Rock, Arkansas, she graduated from the New England Conservatory of Music in 1906. In 1927, Price and her family left Little Rock for Chicago, part of the "Great Migration" of African Americans to the North after World War I. Like so many Black families, the Prices fled Little Rock because of racial violence. The death of a white child supposedly at the hands of an African American man left some people in the white community looking for a Black child to kill in retaliation, and the Price family was prominent enough in Little Rock that their child, Florence Louise Price, was targeted.[2] After struggling to establish herself, Price became a prominent figure in musical circles in Chicago. Black and white women became some of her most important advocates; many performances of her music and other professional opportunities were sponsored by women's musical organizations and patrons. After her Symphony in E minor won the 1932 Wanamaker Prize, the Chicago Symphony Orchestra premiered the piece on a "Negro in Music" concert in June 1933. The concert marked the first time a major American orchestra performed a piece by a Black woman composer. It also featured a Black woman soloist—Margaret Bonds—who played John Alden Carpenter's Concertino for Piano and Orchestra. Yet this historic event was marked by racism. The opening overture "In Old Virginia" was by John Powell, a prominent figure in Virginia who used his significant cultural capital to advocate for the passage of Virginia's eugenics laws in 1924 and founded Anglo-Saxon Clubs to promote the superiority of white folk music.[3]

The third movement of the Symphony in E minor, "Juba Dance" is a rondo and is one of a number of pieces where Price incorporated the characteristic rhythms of the juba, a folk dance originated by enslaved people initially described as "pattin' juba," into her music.[4] Price thought the juba was central to Black music, going so far as to write that "it seems to me to be no more impossible to conceive of Negroid music devoid of the spiritualistic theme on the one hand than strongly syncopated rhythms of the juba on the other."[5] Price evokes the dance in the violin melody and emphasizes rhythm, using the accompanying instruments to mimic the foot-stomping and hand-clapping that is an integral part of the juba.

Rae Linda Brown groups Price with Still and Dawson as composers who worked within an American nationalist style, but their conception of nationalism was so influenced by Black musical traditions that she calls their music Afro-Romantic. Price's musical nationalism stemmed from her own musical experiences. She knew the juba because she was a descendant of enslaved people, and she was familiar with pentatonicism because she had grown up singing spirituals. Price's symphony offers a sonic account of Black experiences in the United States through the entanglements of Black and European musical forms. As part of the Chicago Renaissance (a similar movement to the Harlem Renaissance), Price's use of Black music in concert pieces was a way to infuse Black racial pride into her country's highbrow musical scene. Through her work, Price demonstrated and proclaimed the "validity of black music in the concert hall."[6] Even the subtitle of the Symphony in E Minor, a "Negro Symphony," makes this point.

Rodeo is one of Copland's most famous pieces, and the "Hoe-Down" has become part of American popular culture. Composed for a ballet choreographed by Agnes de Mille, Copland draws on American vernacular music in many sections of the work. "Hoe-Down" quotes a fiddle tune, "Bonyparte," which Copland found in *Our Singing Country*, a folk-music songbook. As Gayle Murchison points out, Copland turned to the "cultural reproduction" of folk-music collections to find suitable tunes to quote in the score because he was not exposed to the kind of vernacular music during his New York childhood that he thought suitable for the pastoral vision presented in the ballet.[7] Although the celebration of the frontier spirit is often associated with conservative American values and whiteness, Elisabeth Crist argues that in the context of the 1930s Leftist ideology that influenced Copland, the West was a more contested space where thinkers questioned the rugged individualism that is such a part of the pioneer myth.[8] The ballet's scenario is about a character named the Cowgirl who has trouble conforming to the gender roles expected of her. In the "hoe-down," however, she bows to convention and puts on a dress for the dance. Although Copland largely quotes the tune of "Bonyparte" intact, his orchestration and playful tonal shifts mark the music as firmly in his style.

It is in the rhythmic language of the two dances that we can most obviously hear the difference between the lineages of the source material. The "Hoe-Down" has a strong emphasis on the downbeat and square rhythms characteristic of many Irish dances that are one of the antecedents of much of Appalachian folk music of which "Bonyparte" is an example. "Juba Dance," on the other hand, features off-beat syncopation and the layered rhythmic patterns of the West African roots of the Juba. Copland's emphasis on harmony reflects the greater value western classical music invests in harmony and melody over rhythm. By using harmonies not typically found in Appalachian fiddle music, Crist suggests that "Copland preserves his own personality while wearing borrowed clothes" much as the Cowgirl does in the ballet.[9] Crist's interpretation is not universally shared by musicologists, with many people seeing the work more as Lynn Garafola describes it: "the quintessential Americana ballet."[10]

The United States conjured by *Rodeo*, and many of Copland's other works, is optimistic, exuberant, and expansionist—a celebration of the wide-open spaces of the West and American exceptionalism. The sort of simplistic nationalism that many people heard in Copland was not universally appreciated, even in wartime America. In 1942, dancer Ted Shawn, upon hearing Copland's music for *Billy the Kid,* protested to Agnes de Mille that "it's because of music like that that we are having war."[11] Despite being smeared in the political sphere in the early 1950s because of his support for Leftist politics, today Copland's music is often featured during patriotic events or when expressions of American national pride are appropriate. For example, the New York Philharmonic performed *The Fanfare for the Common Man* at the dedication for the 9/11 Museum.

Locales & Locations

Price was part of a network of Black women in Chicago who supported each other and overlapped with other networks that championed Black communities and Black empowerment through cultural activities. Black women worked together in a variety of spaces, some rooted in institutions like the church and women's clubs, some more informal such as gatherings that often resembled European salons. Samantha Ege has found that pianist Margaret Bonds and her mother Estella (whose Sunday afternoon musicales were a center of Black Chicago's musical activity), and critics Nora Holt and Maude Roberts George, helped sustain Price emotionally, artistically, and financially. Indeed, Maude George paid the $250 fee to hire the Chicago Symphony to perform at the 1933 "Negro in Music" concert at which the Symphony in E minor was premiered—a concert that was also supported by the Chicago Music Association, a club whose founding president was Nora Holt and whose active membership included Estella Bonds, Maude George, and Price.[12] Copland, on the other hand, was based in New York City and, according to Howard Pollack, was part of an extensive network of gay male musicians and artists who lived there—many of whom eventually achieved national reputations. Because of his prominence, Copland became an important supporter of gay composers (including Virgil Thomson, Marc Blitzstein, and Leonard Bernstein) by championing them through concert series and serving as a liaison with patrons, publishers, and other musicians. Although Copland's homosexuality was not common knowledge outside of artistic circles, the network of which he was a part was central to New York's cultural landscape.[13]

Further Consideration: Work with students to identify the different roles and skills (patrons, performers, concert promoters, concert-venue managers, musicians, etc.) that must be present to produce a vibrant musical scene in a particular place. Challenge them to find some of the people in their community who fill those roles and interview them to understand more about how the local music industry functions.

Forms & Factions

Copland's music has become intertwined with American political nationalism in part because it plays so strongly into American myths that imagine the United States as a largely rural, pastoral (and white) utopia. During his lifetime, Copland was a political progressive, and Elizabeth Crist has demonstrated how this orientation suffuses much of his music.[14] In the early 1950s, his personal politics resulted in a short-lived blacklisting, but today few people have any idea that he and his music were once considered subversive.[15] Emily Ansari argues that the widespread reception of Copland's music as optimistically populist has allowed people from the Left and Right to deploy his music for their own political agendas.[16] The Aaron Copland Fund for Music (which manages the copyrights on the composer's work) resists efforts to use his music in political campaigns. For example, on December 28, 2020, a video celebrating President Donald Trump's accomplishments in office and accompanied by "Hoe-Down" was posted to Trump's personal Twitter account. The Fund immediately protested and the video quickly disappeared.[17] Still, the Fund allows Copland's music to be performed during many patriotic events and licenses it to films, TV shows, and advertisements that use the music to establish an Americana subtext. Price's music (and similar compositions by Black composers), meanwhile, is often interpreted as resisting the domination of a kind of American nationalism that excludes the experiences and perspectives of people of color.

Further Consideration: Ask students to choose a scored excerpt from some form of media (TV, podcast, film, etc.) that they think exemplifies their conception of America. What vision of America is reflected in their choice? What sonic signifiers were important to them in making their choice?

Responses & Reception

During her lifetime, Florence Price had a substantial regional reputation as a composer and was well known in Black classical music circles. After her death, her music vanished from concert programming. When her biographer Rae Linda Brown found a manuscript of Price's third symphony in the archives at Yale University in 1979 (just 26 years after the composer's death), Price had disappeared so thoroughly from musical collective memory that Brown had never heard of her.[18] Even Price herself might have foreseen this erasure because of her experiences as a Black woman in the United States. In a 1943 letter to conductor Serge Koussevitzky, she alludes to these issues when asking him (for a third time) to consider programming her music. She opened the letter with:

> To begin with I have two handicaps—those of sex and race. I am a woman; and I have some Negro blood in my veins. Knowing the worst, then, would you be good enough to hold in check the possible inclination to regard a woman's composition as long on emotionalism but short on virility and thought content;—until you shall have examined some of my work? As to the handicap of race, may I relieve you by saying that I neither expect nor ask any concession on that score. I should like to be judged on merit alone—the great trouble having been to get conductors, who know nothing of my work...to even consent to examine a score.[19]

In her letter, Price identifies the biases against her music that are rooted in stereotypes about race and gender. The same prejudices that impeded her career are also responsible for her erasure. Beginning in about 2010, her work began to be performed by prominent orchestras and musicians as the classical music industry began to respond to long-standing calls to diversify the repertoire.[20] By 2018, the popular press had announced the "rediscovery" of Florence Price and Schirmer announced that they would publish her entire output, much of which was never commercially available during her lifetime. While the resurgence of interest in her music is gratifying, the tiny amount of music by women and people of color programmed in mainstream orchestral and operatic organizations reveals that too often there is little real commitment to diversifying classical music repertoire.[21] Because so little of it is published, it can be very difficult to perform music by historic women and composers of color. As a result, many organizations primarily present newly commissioned music, giving the false impression that people from minoritized communities have only recently started composing classical music.

Further Consideration: Work with your students to locate the scores for a concert of music by historic composers from underrepresented groups.

Notes

1 Richard Taruskin, "Nationalism," *Grove Music Online.*
2 Rae Linda Brown, *The Heart of a Woman: The Life and Music of Florence B. Price* (Urbana: University of Illinois Press, 2020), 77.
3 David Kushner, "John Powell, His Racial and Cultural Ideologies," *Israel Studies in Musicology Online* 5, no. 1 (2006). https://www-biu-ac-il. libproxy.lib.unc.edu/hu/mu/min-ad/index.htm
4 My analysis is dependent upon Rae Linda Brown in *The Heart of a Woman*, 126–45; and "Florence B. Price's 'Negro Symphony,'" in *Temples for Tomorrow: Looking Back at the Harlem Renaissance*, eds. Geneviève Fabre and Michel Feith (Bloomington: Indiana University Press, 2001), 84–98.
5 As quoted in Brown, *The Heart of a Woman*, 131.
6 Brown, *The Heart of a Woman*, 122.
7 Gayle Murchison, "Nationalism in William Grant Still and Aaron Copland between the Wars: Style and Ideology," (Ph.D. diss., Yale University, 1998), 371–72.
8 Elizabeth B. Crist, *Music for the Common Man: Aaron Copland during the Depression and War* (New York: Oxford University Press, 2005), 119.
9 Crist, *Music for the Common Man*, 141. We must also recognize that although the Appalachian fiddle tradition has many influences from musics usually coded as Black, it has been racialized as white in the United States.

10 Lynn Garafola, "Making an American Dance: *Billy the Kid, Rodeo,* and *Appalachian Spring,*" in *Aaron Copland and His World,* eds. Carol J. Oja and Judith Tick (Princeton, NJ: Princeton University Press, 2005), 132.

11 Aaron Copland and Vivian Perlis, *Copland: 1900 through 1942* (Boston: Faber and Faber, 1984), 359 as quoted in Annegret Fauser, *Sounds of War: Music in the United States during World War II* (New York: Oxford University Press, 2013), 160.

12 Samantha Ege, "Composing a Symphonist: Florence Price and the Hand of Black Women's Fellowship," *Women and Music* 24 (2020): 7–27.

13 Howard Pollack, "The Dean of Gay American Composers," *American Music* 18, no. 1 (Spring 2000): 39–49.

14 Crist, *Music for the Common Man.*

15 In 1953, *Lincoln Portrait* was taken off the program for a presidential inauguration concert.

16 See Emily Abrams Ansari, "The Benign American Exceptionalism of Copland's *Fanfare for the Common Man,*" *The Musical Quarterly* 103 (2021): 246–80.

17 Rachel Brodsky, "Aaron Copland Estate Objects to Trump's Use of Late Composer's 'Hoe-Down' in Promotional Video." *The Independent,* December 31, 2020. https://www.independent.co.uk/arts-entertainment/music/news/aaron-copland-hoedown-trump-video-b1780639.html

18 Brown, *The Heart of a Woman,* ix.

19 Brown, *The Heart of a Woman,* 186–87.

20 A cache of her unpublished manuscripts was discovered in an abandoned house in 2009, and the resultant publicity helped to raise Price's profile.

21 See Data Analysis of Orchestral Season, 2019–2020, *Institute for Composer Diversity,* https://www.composerdiversity.com/orchestra-seasons and Sarah Baer, "2020–2021 Season: By the Numbers," *Women's Philharmonic Advocacy,* May 6, 2020, https://wophil.org/202021-by-the-numbers/

Bibliography

Score/Recording (Year of Composition in Parenthesis)

1915–1945

Orchestral

Chavez, Carlos. *Symphony No. 2* (Sinfonia India). New York: G. Schirmer, 1950. (1935–36)

• Orchestra of the Americas. *Copland & Chavez: Pan-American Reflections,* 2019.

Dawson, William. *Negro Folk Symphony.* Delaware Water Gap, PA: Shawnee Press, 1965. (1934, rev. 1952)

• ORF Vienna Radio Symphony Orchestra. *Dawson & Kay: Orchestral Works,* 2020.

Chamber

Bauer, Marion. *Concertino for Oboe, Clarinet and String Quartet*, op. 32b. IMSLP. https://imslp.org/wiki/Concertino_for_Oboe%2C_Clarinet_and_String_Quartet%2C_Op.32b_(Bauer%2C_Marion) (1939)
————. *Duo for Oboe and Clarinet*, op. 25. IMSLP. https://imslp.org/wiki/Duo_for_Oboe_and_Clarinet%2C_Op.25_(Bauer%2C_Marion) (1932)

- Ambache Chamber Orchestra and Ensemble. *Marion Bauer: Orchestral and Chamber Works*, 2005.

Bonis, Mel. *Scènes de la forêt: pour flûte, alto et harpe*. Rheinfelden: Edition Kossack, 2001. (1927/1928)
————. *Suite dans le style ancien: pour flûte, violon, alto et piano*. Rheinfelden: Edition Kossack, 2005. (1928)

- Tatjana Ruhland and Florian Wiek. *La Joueuse de flûte: Romantic Flute Music*, 2006.

Fine, Vivian. *Sonatina for Oboe and Piano*. IMSLP. https://imslp.org/wiki/Sonatina_for_Oboe_and_Piano_(Fine%2C_Vivian) (1942)

- Celeste Johnson. *Wider than the Sky*, 2022.

Kay, Ulysses. *Sonata for Bassoon and Piano*. Medina, NY: Imagine Music Publishing, 2006. (1941)

- Lecolion Washington, Jr. *Legacy: Works for Bassoon by Black Composers*, 2008.

Piano

Ginastera, Alberto. "Pequeña Danza from ballet Estancia." In *The Piano Collection*, edited by Robert Wharton. London: Boosey & Hawkes, 2006. (1941)

- Fernando Viani. *Ginastera: Complete Piano and Organ Music*, 2007.

Song

Price, Florence. "Songs to the Dark Virgin." In *Anthology of Art Songs by Black American Composers*, edited by Willis C. Patterson. New York: Edward B. Marks, 1977. (1941)

- Kevin Maynor. *The Black Art Song*, 2000.

1945–1970

Orchestral

Cordero, Roque. *Concerto for Violin and Orchestra*. New York: Peermusic, 1969. (1962)

- *Black Composers Series*, Vol. 4. Columbia Masterworks, 1974. Remastered by Sony Classical, 2019.

Sowande, Fela. *African Suite: Suite for Strings.* London: Chapell, 1955. (1955)

- CBC Vancouver Chamber Orchestra. *Milhaud, Maurice, Forsyth, Sowande*, 1994.

Orchestra and Solo Instrumental

Bauer, Marion. *American Youth Concerto*, op. 36. IMSLP. https://imslp.org/wiki/American_Youth_Concerto%2C_Op.36_(Bauer%2C_Marion) (1946)

- Ambache Chamber Orchestra and Ensemble. *Marion Bauer: Orchestral and Chamber Works*, 2005.

Chamber

Chou Wen-chung. *Suite for Harp and Wind Quintet.* Leipzig: C. F. Peters, 1951. (1951)

- *From Behind the Unreasoning Mask: Music of Paul Chihara, Chou Wen-chung, Earl Kim, and Roger Reynolds*, 1998.

Lutyens, Elisabeth. *Fantasie-Trio*, op. 55. Heslington: University of York Music Press, 2003. (1963)
———. *String Trio*, op. 57. London: Schott, 1964. (1964)

- Exaudi; Endymion. *Lutyens: A Centennial Celebration*, 2006.

Perry, Julia. *Homunculus, C.F.* In *New Historical Anthology of Music by Women*, edited by James R. Briscoe. Bloomington: Indiana University Press, 2004. (1960)

- Manhattan Percussion Ensemble. *Harrison: Suite for Percussion; Perry: Homunculus, C.F.; Gyring: Piano Sonata No. 2*, 2010.

Piano

Barbosa, Cacilda Borges. *Estudos brasileiros para piano.* São Paulo: Ricordi Brasileira. IMSLP. https://imslp.org/wiki/Estudos_brasileiros_para_piano_(Barbosa,_Cacilda_Borges) (1965)

- Beatriz Balzi, Recording. YouTube. https://www.youtube.com/watch?v=Dm3-Bssqt6Lg

Bonds, Margaret. "Troubled Water." In *Black Women Composers: A Century of Piano Music (1893–1990)*, edited by Helen Walker-Hill. Bryn Mawr, PA: Hildegard Publishing, 1992. (1967).

- Samantha Ege. *Four Women: Music for Solo Piano by Price, Kaprálová, Bilsland and Bonds*, 2018.

Ginastera, Alberto. Rondo on Argentine Folk Tunes (1947), Sonata No. 1, op. 22 (1952), Suite de Danzas Criollas (1946). In *The Piano Collection*, edited by Robert Wharton. London: Boosey & Hawkes, 2006.

- Fernando Viani. *Ginastera: Complete Piano and Organ Music*, 2007.

Guarnieri, M. Camargo. *Sonatina No. 6*. New York: Associated Music Publishers, 1973. (1965)

- *A Música para Piano: Camargo Guarnieri*, 2014.

Vocal Chamber Music

Gideon, Miriam. *The Hound of Heaven*. New York: Columbia University Music Press, 1975. (1945)
———. *Rhymes from the Hill*. Hillsdale, NY: Mobart Music Publications, 1968. (1966)

- Prism Orchestra. *Music of Miriam Gideon: Vocal Chamber Works*, 1998.

Perry, Julia. *Stabat Mater*. New York: Southern Music Publishing Company, 1954. (1951)

- Japan Philharmonic Symphony Orchestra. *Moore: Symphony in A; Perry: Stabat Mater*, 2010.

Choral

Kay, Ulysses. *O Praise the Lord: Psalm 117*. New York: C. F. Peters, 1961. (1961)

- Trinity Church Choir. *Music from Trinity Church Wall Street, Vol. 1*, 1989.

1970–2000

Opera

Davis, Anthony. *X: The Life and Times of Malcolm X*. New York: G. Schirmer, 1986. (1986)

- *X: The Life and Times of Malcolm X: An Opera in Three Acts*, 1992.

Orchestral

Takemitsu, Tōru. *A Flock Descends into the Pentagonal Garden*. Editions Salabert, 2002. (1977)

- Bournemouth Symphony Orchestra. *Takemitsu: A Flock Descends into the Pentagonal Garden*, 2006.

———. *Archipelago S*. New York: Schott, 1994. (1993)
———. *Dream/Window*. New York: Schott, 1988. (1985)
———. *How Slow the Wind*. New York: Schott, 1994. (1991)

————. *Twill by Twilight: In Memory of Morton Feldman.* New York: Schott, 1989. (1988)

————. *Quotation of Dream: Say Sea, Take Me!* Tokyo: Schott Japan, 2000. (1991)

- London Sinfonietta. *Takemitsu: Quotation of Dream*, 1998.

Chamber

Anderson, Thomas Jefferson (T.J.). *Intermezzi.* Berlin: Bote & Bock, 1985. (1983)

- Videmus. *Works by T.J. Anderson, David Baker, Donal Fox, and Olly Wilson*, 2007.

Kaneko, Hitomi. *Miyabi.* Mainz, Germany: Schott. (1991)

- Ewa Liebchen and Rafał Jędrzejewski. Recording. YouTube. https://www.youtube.com/watch?v=1KKzi9QF46k

Moore, Dorothy Rudd. *Night Fantasy for Clarinet and Piano.* New York: American Composers Alliance, 1979. (1978)

- Marcus Eleu. *But Not Forgotten: Music by African-American Composers for Clarinet and Piano*, 2012.

Takemitsu, Tōru. *Signals from Heaven: Two Antiphonal Fanfares.* Tokyo: Schott Japan, 2006. (1987)

- London Sinfonietta. *Takemitsu: Quotation of Dream*, 1998.

Tan Dun. *Eight Colors for String Quartet.* New York: G. Schirmer, 1988. (1986–88)

- Arditti String Quartet. *Tan Dun: Snow in June*, 2007.

Wilson, Olly. *A City Called Heaven.* Milwaukee: Shawnee Press, n.d. (1988)

- Thamyris. *A City Called Heaven*, 2002.

Piano

Ginastera, Alberto. Sonata no. 2, op. 53 (1981, rev. 1983), Sonata no. 3, op. 55 (1982). In *The Piano Collection*, edited by Robert Wharton. London: Boosey & Hawkes, 2006.

- Fernando Viani. *Ginastera: Complete Piano and Organ Music*, 2007.

Orchestra & Voice

Walker, George. *Lilacs for Voice and Orchestra.* Vocal/piano reduction. St, Louis: Lauren Keiser Publishing, n.d. (1995)

- Ian Hobson. *George Walker: Great American Orchestral Works*, Vol. 4, 2014.

Vocal Chamber

Gideon, Miriam. *The Resounding Lyre.* Hillsdale, NY: Mobart Music, 1983. (1979)
————. *Spirit above the Dust: A Song Cycle on American Poetry.* New York: Peters, 1981. (1981)
————. *Wing'd Hour (A Song Cycle).* New York: Peters, 1985. (1983)
   • Prism Orchestra. *Music of Miriam Gideon: Vocal Chamber Works,* 1998.

Song

Moore, Undine Smith. "Is There Anybody Here That Loves My Jesus." In *Art Songs and Spirituals by African-American Women Composers,* edited by Vivian Taylor. Bryn Mawr, PA: Hildegard Publishing Company, 1995. (1981)
   • Oral Moses. *Sankofa: A Spiritual Reflection,* 2019.

2000–present

Opera

Du Yun. *Angel's Bone.* New York: G. Schirmer, 2015. (2015)
   • *Angel's Bone,* 2017.

Orchestral

Nishimura, Akira. *Melodies from Light and Shadow.* Tokyo: Zen-on Music, 2001. (2000)
   • NHK Symphony Orchestra. *Karura: Orchestra Works by Akira Nishimura,* 2002.

Chamber

Chen Yi. *Night Thoughts.* King of Prussia, PA: Theodore Presser, 2004. (2004)
   • Meininger Trio. *Voices of the Rainforest,* 2011

Fábregas, Elisenda. *Voices of the Rainforest.* Leipzig: F. Hofmeister, 2009. (2008)
   • Meininger Trio. *Voices of the Rainforest,* 2011.

Larsen, Libby. *Slow Structures.* Minneapolis: Libby Larsen Publishing; Kenwood Editions, 2015. (2005)
   • Meininger Trio. *Voices of the Rainforest,* 2011

Piano

Ndodana-Breen, Bongani. "Flowers in the Sand." In *Piano Music of Africa and the African Diaspora*, Volume 4, compiled and edited by William H. Chapman Nyaho. New York: Oxford University Press, 2008.

- • William Chapman Nyaho. *Asa: Piano Music by Composers of African Descent, Volume 2*, 2008.

Selected Secondary Sources

Bailey, Ben E. "Opera/South: A Brief History." *The Black Perspective in Music* 13, no. 1 (1985): 48–78.

Banfield, William C. *Musical Landscapes in Color: Conversations with Black American Composers*. Lanham, MD: Scarecrow Press, 2003.

- • Interviews with Black composers including T.J. Anderson, George Walker, Dorothy Rudd Moore, Olly Wilson, and Anthony Davis.

Barg, Lisa. "Paul Robeson's *Ballad for Americans*: Race and the Cultural Politics of 'People's Music.'" *Journal of the Society of American Music* 2, no. 1 (February 2008): 27–70.

Béhague, Gerard. "Indianism in Latin American Art-Music Composition of the 1920s to 1940s: Case Studies from Mexico, Peru, and Brazil." *Latin American Music Review / Revista de Música Latinoamericana* 27, no. 1 (2006): 28–37.

Bryan, Karen M. "Clarence Cameron White's *Ouanga!* in the World of the Harlem Renaissance." In *Blackness in Opera*, edited by Naomi André, Karen M. Bryan, and Eric Saylor, 116–40. Urbana: University of Illinois Press, 2012.

Callam, Katie A., Makiko Kimoto, Misako Ohta, and Carol J. Oja. "Marian Anderson's 1953 Concert Tour of Japan: A Transnational History." *American Music* 37, no. 3 (Fall 2019): 266–329.

Chybowski, Julia J. "Selling Musical Taste in Early Twentieth-Century America: Frances E. Clark and the Business of Music Appreciation." *Journal of Historical Research in Music Education* 38, no. 2 (2017): 104–27.

Collins, Nick, and Julio d'Escriván, eds. *The Cambridge Companion to Electronic Music*. Cambridge: Cambridge University Press, 2017.

Floyd, Samuel A., Jr. "Troping the Blues: From Spirituals to the Concert Hall." *Black Music Research Journal* 13, no. 1 (1993): 31–51.

Ghuman, Nalini. "'Persian Composer-Pianist Baffles': Kaikhosru Sorabji." In *Western Music and Race*, edited by Julie Brown, 125–44. Cambridge: Cambridge University Press, 2007.

Gidal, Marc. "Contemporary 'Latin American' Composers of Art Music in the United States: Cosmopolitans Navigating Multiculturalism and Universalism." *Latin American Music Review / Revista de Música Latinoamericana* 31, no. 1 (2010): 40–78.

Gutkin, David. "The Modernities of H. Lawrence Freeman." *Journal of the American Musicological Society* 72, no. 3 (2019): 719–79.

Hoven, Lena van der and Liani Maasdorp, "'Opera is an Art for Everyone': Black Empowerment in the South African Opera Adaptations *Unogumbe* (2013) and *Breathe—Umphefumlo* (2015)." In *African Theatre 19: Opera & Music Theatre*, edited by Christine Matzke, Lena van der Hoven, Christopher Odhiambo, and Hilde Roos, 52–76. Woodbridge: James Currey, 2020. [adaptations of Britten's *Noye's Fludde* and *La Bohème*]

Hung, Eric. "Performing 'Chineseness' on the Western Concert Stage: The Case of Lang Lang." *Asian Music* 40, no. 1 (2009): 131–48.

Kelly, Jennifer. *In Her Own Words: Conversations with Composers in the United States.* Urbana: University of Illinois Press, 2013.

- Interviews with women composers including Chen Yi and Libby Larsen

Locke, Ralph P. and Cyrilla Barr, eds. *Cultivating Music in America: Women Patrons and Activists since 1860.* Berkeley: University of California Press, 1997.

- Cyrilla Barr, "A Style of Her Own: The Patronage of Elizabeth Sprague Coolidge," 185–203.
- Doris Evans McGinty, "'As Large as She Can Make It': The Role of Black Women Activists in Music, 1880–1945," 214–36.
- Carol J. Oja, "Women and Patrons and Crusaders for Modernist Music: New York in the 1920s," 237–61.
- Ruth A. Solie, "Culture, Feminism, and the Sacred: Sophie Drinker's Musical Activism," 266–89.

Miller, Leta E. and J. Michele Edwards. *Chen-Yi.* Urbana: University of Illinois Press, 2020.

- Guide to her life and works with chapters divided by performing forces

Oh, Hee Sook. "Intercultural Aesthetics in the Contemporary Korean Compositions of Hae-Sung Lee." *The World of Music*, n.s., 6, no. 1 (2017): 103–22.

Omojola, Bode. "Black Diasporic Encounters: A Study of the Music of Fela Sowande." *Black Music Research Journal* 27, no. 2 (2007): 141–70.

Park, Hye-Jung. "Musical Entanglements: Ely Haimowitz and Orchestral Music under the US Army Military Government in Korea, 1945–1948." *Journal of the Society for American Music* 51, no. 1 (2021) 1–29.

Saavedra, Leonora. "Staging the Nation: Race, Religion and History in Mexican Opera of the 1940s." *Opera Quarterly* 23, no. 1 (2007): 1–21.

Sadoh, Godwin. "African Musicology: A Bibliographical Guide to Nigerian Art Music (1927–2009)." *Notes*, 2nd ser., 66, no. 3 (2010): 485–502.

Scherzinger, Martin. "'Art' Music in a Cross-Cultural Context: The Case of Africa." In *The Cambridge History of Twentieth-Century Music*, edited by Nicholas Cook and Anthony Pople, 584–613. Cambridge: Cambridge University Press, 2004.

Schmalenberger, Sarah. "Debuting Her Political Voice: The Lost Opera of Shirley Graham." *Black Music Research Journal* 26, no. 1 (Spring 2006): 39–87.

Schwartz-Kates, Deborah. "Alberto Ginastera, Argentine Cultural Construction, and the *Gauchesco* Tradition." *The Musical Quarterly* 86, no. 2 (2002): 248–81.

Walker-Hill, Helen. *From Spirituals to Symphonies: African-American Women Composers and Their Music.* Urbana: University of Illinois Press, 2007.

- Chapters on individual composers including Undine Smith Moore, Julia Perry, Margaret Bonds, and Dorothy Rudd Moore

Index

Note: **Bold** page numbers refer to tables; *italic* page numbers refer to musical examples and page numbers followed by "n" denote endnotes.

Printed and bound by CPI Group (UK) Ltd, Croydon, CR0 4YY

01/12/2024

01797771-0005